SQL SYMPHONY

Harmonizing Data Analytics

Oladeji Afolabi

SQL Symphony

Copyright © 2023 by **Oladeji Afolabi**

CONTENTS

INTRODUCTION

H ey, have you ever been on the edge of a bustling city, just taking in all the sights and sounds of the world around you? Picture this: blaring horns, screeching brakes, the hum of conversation, all coming together in a wild symphony. It's chaos, but it's also strangely beautiful. You can't help but be amazed at how everything somehow coordinates into this harmonious mess.

Now, here's a thought: what if we could take that same power and apply it to something unexpected? Like, say, data. I know, I know. Data doesn't sound very exciting. But trust me, within that world of numbers and figures lies a symphony waiting to be conducted. And that symphony has the potential to change the game in our data-driven world.

Welcome to "SQL Symphony: Harmonizing Data Analytics." In this book, I'll take you on a journey through the realm of data-driven decision-making. Whether you're a newbie trying to figure out what the heck data analysis even means, or a seasoned pro looking to brush up your skills, I got you covered. Get ready to become a master of SQL and turn complex data analytics into something accessible and hands-on.

Imagine this: you're standing on a massive stage, surrounded by a team of data analysts and decision-makers. The conductor lifts his baton, and with a flick of his wrist, the symphony begins. Each section of the orchestra represents a different aspect of data analytics, and they all play their own unique melody. The querying section sets the rhythm, extracting raw data with pinpoint precision. The transforming section adds depth and complexity, shaping the data into a beautiful composition. And finally, the visualizing section paints a picture, turning something intangible into something that you can actually see and understand.

But this symphony isn't just a show. It's an experience. It's a chance for you to dive headfirst into the world of data analysis and discover the magic of SQL. Throughout this book, we'll tackle real-world projects that challenge and inspire you. We'll unravel intricate business problems and uncover hidden patterns in massive datasets. By the end, you'll be confidently wielding the power of SQL, ready to conquer the data-driven landscape.

But why should you even care about data analysis and SQL? In a world where information is everything, being able to find meaningful insights in mountains of data is not just a valuable skill – it's a necessary one. Whether you're a business leader making important decisions, a marketer trying to understand your customers, or just someone who wants to uncover hidden gems, "SQL Symphony" will give you the tools and knowledge you need to navigate the data-driven world.

But let me tell you, "SQL Symphony" is not your average dry, technical manual. It's an adventure. It's a journey that will excite your curiosity and push the limits of what you think is possible. We're going to weave together storytelling and science, uncovering patterns hidden beneath the surface and insights that can change the game for businesses and industries.

So, here's the big question: are you ready to compose your very own data symphony? Are you ready to harmonize insights and make a real difference in the data-driven world? If you are, then let's start the "SQL Symphony." Let's go on this thrilling journey together as we discover the power of SQL and turn data analytics into something exciting, captivating, and ultimately transformative. Get ready to take a front row seat in the grand orchestra of data-driven decision-making. The stage is set, the baton is raised, and the symphony is about to begin. Will you join me?

CHAPTER 1

ORCHESTRATING DATA ANALYTICS

Welcome to SQL Symphony

This book is like a guiding light to sail through the vast ocean of structured query language (SQL) and its impact on data analytics. It's meticulously crafted with the desire to enlighten and empower, giving you the keys to unlock the power of SQL. Trust me, it's like a compass leading you through this maze.

Now, before we dive into the nitty-gritty of SQL, we need to lay the foundation for this whole symphony. We got to understand where it all started and why it's so darn important in today's world of data analysis. Think of this introduction like an overture, setting the stage for the knowledge feast that's about to begin.

So, let's go back to the 1970s, an era when IBM researchers, Donald D. Chamberlin and Raymond F. Boyce, had a vision. They wanted to make accessing and managing data stored in databases easier and more efficient. And yes, they did succeed! Their groundbreaking research introduced the relational model, the very cornerstone of SQL. It's basically a framework that lets you organize, query, and manipulate data like a pro.

Now, fast forward to the present, and SQL has become the go-to language in data analytics. It's like a secret code spoken by programmers, data scientists, analysts, and database administrators. With the explosion of data in recent years, SQL has become even more critical, like an essential tool to unlock all those hidden treasures buried in the digital landscape.

SQL, which stands for Structured Query Language, is the guiding star in the vast galaxy of data analytics. Think of it as the master key that unlocks the treasures hidden within data. SQL is the language that empowers you to effortlessly organize, retrieve, and transform data, making it your trusty companion in the world of data analysis. It's the secret code shared among tech professionals, allowing them to navigate and command the rich data landscape of today's digital world with finesse and precision.

So, what's the deal with this book, you ask? Well, it has two main goals. First, it wants to demystify SQL. It doesn't matter if you're a rookie or a seasoned pro, this book has got something for you. It is like a SQL crash course, equipping you with the knowledge and skills to navigate the ever-changing world of data analytics.

The second goal? This book wants to open your eyes to the immense potential of SQL. It's a guide that shows you how to turn raw data into valuable and actionable insights. Trust me, when you master SQL, you gain the power to manipulate and analyze data like a virtuoso. You can merge tables, dig deep into complex analyses, and uncover those hidden patterns that were just begging to be found.

But before we can truly appreciate the beauty of SQL, we need to understand its core principles. You see, SQL is a declarative language. It's not just about telling the computer how to do stuff—it's about describing what we want from our data. And that's where the simplicity and elegance of SQL shine through. It's an accessible tool that turns tables into a world of wonders. Each column holds distinct characteristics, while each row reveals unique records. It's like a vessel filled with endless possibilities.

But here's the real kicker—SQL's true strength lies in its ability to manipulate those tables with grace and precision. Through well-crafted queries, you can select specific data, filter out the noise, and perform mind-bending calculations. And it doesn't stop there! SQL lets you combine tables, merge their contents, and dig out those hidden narratives buried deep within your databases. It's like playing a symphony—the queries are the melodious notes, and the analyses are the harmonious arrangements.

And guess who's going to be our conductor through this symphony of data? SQL, of course! It's going to guide us through each movement, each part of the data analysis process. From the basics of querying and filtering to those fancy statistical analyses, SQL Symphony will arm you with the knowledge and skills to compose your own data-driven masterpiece.

So, I invite you to join me on this thrilling journey through the SQL Symphony. It's going to blow your mind, captivate your senses, and ignite your curiosity. Together, we'll unravel the mysteries of SQL, explore its depths, and embrace its transformative powers like never before.

Why SQL Is the Conductor of Data Analytics

You know, after years of being knee-deep in software development and data analysis, I've really come to understand just how vital SQL is in the world of data. SQL, or Structured Query Language for those not in the know, is like the secret sauce that makes data analysis work. It's like the conductor of a symphony, bringing all the elements together in perfect harmony.

Seriously, SQL is the bridge between raw data and the actionable insights we're all after. Without it, data analysis would be an absolute mess - like trying to solve a Rubik's Cube blindfolded. Let me give you an example to really illustrate why SQL is such a big deal.

Let's say there's this retail company that wants to up their game by digging into their sales data. They've got databases full of sales transactions, customer info, and product details. To make sense of it all, they need to do some fancy footwork with the data - filtering, aggregating, and joining it together. And that's where SQL swoops in, superhero-style.

With SQL, they can write queries to extract exactly what they need. Want to analyze sales transactions from the past year for a specific customer segment? Boom, SQL's got that covered. It's like teleporting straight to the relevant subset of data, which makes the analysis way more manageable and focused.

But SQL doesn't stop there. Oh no, it's got more tricks up its sleeve. Once the data's been pulled, SQL lets the company do all kinds of calculations and aggregations. They can figure out total sales revenue, average order size, customer lifetime value - you name it. These numbers give them insights into their financial performance, customer preferences, and areas that could use some love. And SQL's got this insane library of mathematical and statistical functions to make it super precise and accurate.

Here's where it gets really juicy. SQL also plays matchmaker and brings together data from different sources. That retail company, for instance, might have their sales data, customer info, and product details all in separate databases. But SQL's not about to let them stay apart. It can combine them all into one giant data feast for analysis. It's like you suddenly discover connections and patterns that were invisible before. For example, they could mix sales data with product attributes to see what features make customers go gaga.

But you know what's really cool about SQL? It's like the Spiderman of data analysis - anyone can use it, no radioactive spider bite required. Its simple, user-friendly syntax makes it accessible to techies and non-techies alike. This means data analysts, business folks, and the big shots can all jump in and play around with the data. They don't have to rely so heavily on IT or data engineering teams, which is a game-changer. It creates a culture where decisions are driven by data, and everyone has access to the critical insights they need.

But wait, there's more! SQL isn't just a one-trick pony. It also knows a thing or two about keeping data safe and sound. In this age of data privacy and compliance, we can't just let our data run wild. We need a tool that can keep it under lock and key. That's where SQL comes in handy with its top-notch security features.

Think user authentication, access controls, audit trails - all the good stuff. With SQL, organizations can protect their sensitive data and make sure only the right people can access and fiddle with it.

So, to wrap it all up, SQL is the rockstar conductor of data analytics. It brings order to the chaos and makes sense of the jumble of data we swim in. Extracting, manipulating, and analyzing data wouldn't be the same without it. And as our data keeps growing by leaps and bounds, SQL will be there, leading the charge to uncover its hidden potential. It's like the Tony Stark of the data world - smart, reliable, and always ready to save the day.

CHAPTER 2

SQL OVERTURE

Fundamentals of SQL

As I delve into the vast landscape of SQL, I can't help but be mesmerized by the way this language navigates the realm of data analytics. SQL, or Structured Query Language, holds incredible power and is widely embraced for its ability to organize, access, and manipulate data in relational databases. It's the heartbeat of developers and data analysts alike.

To fully grasp the concept of SQL, we need to understand its basic building blocks. SQL operates within the world of relational databases, where data is stored in tables, neatly arranged in rows and columns. Each table represents a specific entity or object that we're eager to explore. Imagine a database for a retail store, with separate tables for customers, products, and sales.

Creating a table in SQL is like sculpting a work of art. We employ the CREATE TABLE statement to breathe life into our table, naming it and defining the columns it will house, along with their respective data types. Each column becomes an attribute, a distinctive characteristic of the entity we're focusing on. In the case of a customer table, we might have columns like name, address, and phone number.

Once the table is brought to life, we can infuse it with data using the INSERT statement. With this powerful command, we easily provide values for each column, fashioning rows of tangible data.

For instance, to add a new customer to our table, we simply specify their name, address, and phone number.

Now, let's dive into the excitement of querying data with the SELECT statement. This command opens the door to a world of possibilities, allowing us to retrieve specific columns or records that meet certain criteria. Using SELECT, we can filter, sort, and join data from multiple tables to unlock invaluable insights. Picture extracting details like all customers living in a specific city or calculating the total sales for a particular product.

The structure of a SELECT statement is a wondrous symphony. Its melodious clauses harmonize to craft our desired result. At its core, we have the SELECT clause, where we specify the columns we want to retrieve. Then, the FROM clause enters the stage, indicating which table(s) we want to query. Want to add more depth to the composition? We can employ the WHERE clause to filter rows based on conditions, the ORDER BY clause to arrange the outcome, and the GROUP BY clause to categorize the result by one or more columns. Here is a simple SQL code for this:

```
```
-- First, let's filter customers living in a specific city.
SELECT CustomerName, City
FROM Customers
WHERE City = 'YourCityName';

-- Next, let's calculate the total sales for a particular product.
SELECT ProductName, SUM(Quantity * UnitPrice) AS TotalSales
FROM Products
JOIN OrderDetails ON Products.ProductID = OrderDetails.ProductID
WHERE ProductName = 'YourProductName'
GROUP BY ProductName;
```
```

But SQL's spellbinding capabilities don't stop at querying. We can also modify and update data using the UPDATE statement. This command enables us to change the values of specific columns in one or more rows, driven by predefined conditions. Imagine updating a customer's phone number if it has changed over time, keeping our records accurate and up to date.

Just like a scene in a suspenseful movie, SQL introduces the DELETE statement. With this command, we can eliminate specific rows that meet certain conditions. Imagine removing the records of customers who have not made a purchase in the last year, decluttering our database and focusing on the customers truly engaged with our products.

But wait, there's more! Constraints steal the spotlight, ensuring the integrity and consistency of our precious data. They enforce rules on columns, demanding a certain format for a phone number or guaranteeing a unique value for a primary key. Constraints serve as guardians, preserving the cleanliness and reliability of our data.

As we embark on this journey into the depths of SQL, we discover its advanced capabilities for data manipulation and analysis. We are introduced to the powerful ensemble of aggregate functions like SUM, COUNT, AVG, and MAX. These functions allow us to perform calculations on groups of data, giving us access to valuable statistics and uncovering hidden insights.

SQL's versatility thrives in complex calculations and transformations. Prepare to be enchanted by subqueries, derived tables, and views. Subqueries enable us to nest queries within queries, unraveling intricate layers of data retrieval. Derived tables act as magical creations, allowing us to establish temporary tables based on query results, simplifying and organizing our complex inquiries. And views, ah views, they are virtual tables derived from queries, serving as separate entities and unlocking patterns of data retrieval.

SQL presents a lush garden of operators and functions for data transformation and manipulation. We're bestowed with the power of mathematical operators to perform arithmetic miracles, comparison operators to dance between values, and string functions to entwine threads of text. Date and time functions whisk us into a realm where we traverse temporal landscapes, while logical operators weave conditions together.

As I reflect on the grand design of SQL, I'm filled with awe and deep appreciation for its elegance in handling data. To truly master SQL, we must not only comprehend its syntax and capabilities, but also embrace a creative mindset to channel its power effectively. SQL Symphony awaits us, an invigorating invitation to explore this harmonious language and unleash its true potential in the realm of data analytics. It serves as a symphony that gives life to data, transforming it into meaningful insights that drive innovation and growth.

Setting Up Your SQL Environment

So, here's the deal. You're diving headfirst into the world of data analytics, right? Before we get into the nitty-gritty technical stuff, let's take a step back and really understand what SQL is all about. I mean, it's going to be your go-to language for managing and manipulating databases, so trust me, you want to know what's up.

So, SQL, or Structured Query Language, is basically a programming language that's specifically designed for dealing with databases. It's like the glue that holds everything together. With SQL, you can store, retrieve, and analyze data like a boss. It's standardized and efficient, which is mega important when you're dealing with loads of data.

But first things first, you got to choose the right SQL platform for your needs. I mean, there are so many options out there! You've got MySQL, PostgreSQL, Oracle, and Microsoft SQL Server, just to name a few.

Among the realm of data platforms, there's one that stands apart—BigQuery. While it's a platform that's no stranger to the world of SQL, it doesn't quite fit the traditional mold of relational database management systems (RDBMS) like MySQL, PostgreSQL, Oracle, or Microsoft SQL Server. BigQuery is something of a maverick, specializing in handling vast datasets and conducting intricate analytical queries. Its primary focus is on data warehousing and analytics, making it a key player in the cloud-based data world. So, while it shares the language of SQL, it dances to its own tune in the realm of data, operating in a distinct context from the RDBMS.

Here, we will focus on MySQL 'cause it's open-source, super popular, and great for newbies.

As a beginner, you may want an online platform to practice your SQL. SQL Fiddle is one of such available options. It is an online SQL sandbox that allows you to practice SQL queries with various database systems, including MySQL. It's a great platform for experimenting with SQL without the need for local installations.

Alright, let's get MySQL installed, shall we?

Step 1 is to download MySQL Community Server from their official website. Easy peasy, just head to https://www.mysql.com/downloads/ and pick the version that matches your operating system. Once that's done, run the installer and let the magic happen.

Next up, the MySQL Installation Wizard is going to guide you through the process. Just follow the directions on your screen and choose the installation type that works best for you. If you're new to all this, I'd recommend going with the "Typical" installation. It's got all the basics you need to get started with your SQL environment.

During the installation, you'll come across some configuration settings. Stuff like installation path, server type, and port number. Now, the default values are usually fine for beginners, but if you want to get fancy, feel free to tweak them to your heart's content.

After all that, it's time to set up a user account. You're going to be the root user, the big cheese, the one with all the power. So, choose a strong password 'cause you don't want any sneaky hackers messing with your data, do you?

Once the installation is complete and your user account is all set up, you have the option to start the MySQL server as a Windows service. This basically means that your SQL environment will always be available, even when your machine starts up. It's just more convenient that way, trust me.

Alright, so now that you've got MySQL up and running, it's time to really make it work for you.

Step 1 of the configuration process is to mess around with the my.ini/my.cnf file. This file holds all the settings that make MySQL tick. You can find it in the installation directory, and you just got to open it up with a text editor. From there, you can tweak things like memory allocation, connection limits, and where log files are saved. If you're not sure what to do, check out the MySQL documentation or ask a pro.

To actually start playing around with your databases, you got to launch the MySQL Command-Line Client. It's like the control center for all your SQL goodness. So, head to the MySQL installation directory, find the "bin" folder, and open up a command prompt. Type in "MySQL" followed by the right options and arguments, and bam! You're logged into the MySQL server.

Now you're ready to start creating databases and tables. The CREATE DATABASE statement is your BFF when it comes to making new databases, and the CREATE TABLE statement lets you define the structure of your tables. Make sure you know a thing or two about database design and the different data types supported by SQL. You want your tables to be efficient and organized, after all.

Oh, and don't forget about importing data into your beautiful new tables. This is where the magic of SQL really starts to shine. MySQL gives you a bunch of ways to do it, like using SQL statements, CSV files, or external tools. The LOAD DATA INFILE statement is perfect for importing data from a CSV, while the INSERT statement lets you add one row at a time. Do whatever works best for you and your juicy data.

And guess what? Now that you've got everything set up and your data imported, you're all set to start querying. Time to unleash the full power of SQL for some serious data analysis. You've got a whole arsenal of commands at your disposal, but the SELECT statement is where it's at. Use SELECT to get exactly what you need - columns, tables, conditions, you name it. To write really killer queries, make sure you understand SQL syntax and how to optimize your queries for top-notch performance.

So there you have it! You've now set up your SQL environment and you're ready to dive headfirst into the exciting world of data analytics. By following the steps I've laid out for you, you've got MySQL installed and configured, ready to crunch those numbers. Don't forget to keep your SQL environment super secure with strong passwords, and have fun exploring the incredible world of data analytics with the power of SQL.

Executing Your SQL Query

Alright, before we jump into the exercises, let's get a grasp on what exactly a SQL query is. It's basically a fancy statement written in the SQL language that lets you retrieve or manipulate data from a super cool database. It's like your secret language for communicating with the database and getting what you want from it, you know?

So, let's start our little adventure with a simple exercise. Picture this, you're working on this super important project where you need to keep track of all the employees in a company. Let's call this database "EmployeeDB," catchy name, right? And to create this database, all you got to do is use this nifty SQL query:

```
CREATE DATABASE EmployeeDB;
```

Boom! Executing this query means you've successfully created a brand spanking' new database called "EmployeeDB." High five!

Now that we've got our database set up, let's move on to the next step and create a table within this database to store all that juicy employee information. We'll call this table "Employees." To create this table, just throw this SQL query in there:

```
CREATE TABLE Employees (
   EmployeeID INT,
   FirstName VARCHAR(50),
   LastName VARCHAR(50),
   Age INT,
   Department VARCHAR(50)
);
```

And there you have it! By executing this query, you'll have a cool table called "Employees" with nifty columns for EmployeeID, FirstName, LastName, Age, and Department. Each of these columns has its own special data type, like INT for numbers and VARCHAR for strings.

Alright, now that we've gotten ourselves a sweet database and table, let's kick it up a notch and add some data to our Employees table. And to do that, we'll be using the INSERT INTO statement. It's like the key to adding new records to a table. Check it out:

```
INSERT INTO Employees (EmployeeID, FirstName, LastName,
Age, Department)
VALUES (1, 'John', 'Doe', 25, 'Sales');
```

Sweet! By executing this query, we've just added a super cool employee named John Doe to the Employees table. You can do this over and over again to add more employees, changing up the values each time to make it more interesting.

Now that we've got our database, our table, and some awesome data in it, it's time for the big moment. We're going to run our first SQL query to retrieve some information from the Employees table.

Get ready, 'cause this is where the real magic happens. We're going to use the SELECT statement for this bad boy. The SELECT statement lets us ask the database for specific data based on what we're looking' for.

Let's say we're curious about all the employees in the Sales department. Well, our SQL query would look a little something' like this:

```
```
SELECT * FROM Employees WHERE Department = 'Sales';
```
```

Bam! Executing this query means we'll get a fancy result set that includes all the records from the Employees table where the Department column says 'Sales.' The asterisk (*) in the SELECT clause means we want to grab all the columns. But hey, if you only want specific columns, you can swap out that asterisk for the column names you fancy.

Hold onto your seat, 'cause we're not done yet. SQL queries aren't just about fetching data, we can also do some pretty nifty calculations and aggregations with them. Let's say we want to know the average age of all the salespeople. No problem! Just combine the SELECT statement with the AVG function, like this:

```
```
SELECT AVG(Age) FROM Employees WHERE Department = 'Sales';
```
```

Boom! Executing this query gives us the average age of our sales heroes. The AVG function does all the dirty work, calculating the average value of the Age column for all the records that satisfy the WHERE clause. Pretty neat, huh?

As you gain more experience with SQL queries, you'll start to discover all sorts of fancy functions and operators that let you do cool stuff with your data. From simple calculations to mind-blowing analytics, SQL is a powerhouse of tools to help you work magic with your data.

To really solidify what we've learned so far, let's dive into a few more practical examples. First up, finding employees who are older than 30. Easy peasy, lemon squeezy:

```
SELECT FirstName, LastName FROM Employees WHERE Age > 30;
```

Next, let's retrieve the number of employees in each department. Fancy pantsy, here we go:

```
SELECT Department, COUNT(*) FROM Employees GROUP BY Department;
```

Now let's say we want to update the age of an employee with ID 2, to 35. It's like a magic spell, watch this:

```
UPDATE Employees SET Age = 35 WHERE EmployeeID = 2;
```

And finally, let's imagine we want to delete all employees from the IT department. Goodbye, IT peeps!

```
DELETE FROM Employees WHERE Department = 'IT';
```

Wowza! By working on these examples and playing around with different SQL queries, you'll gain some real hands-on experience and start feeling like a SQL master. Practice makes perfect, and SQL is no exception.

Finally, running your very first SQL query is a big moment in your journey towards becoming an awesome data analyst. We've gone through some fun exercises and examples together, getting you all prepped to write and execute your very own SQL queries. So now, let's embrace the power of SQL and go on this amazing adventure together, unlocking all the secrets it holds for our data analytics symphony. Let's make some magic happen!

CHAPTER 3

SQL CRESCENDO – DATA RETRIEVAL

SELECT Statements: Extracting Data

So, you're working with a database, huh? And let me guess, it's got a ton of columns, right? Well, lucky for you, you don't have to retrieve all that data. I mean, who's got time for that? You can use this nifty little thing called the SELECT statement to specify which columns you want to retrieve. It's like a filtering system that not only reduces the amount of data you get but also makes your queries faster. Talk about hitting two birds with one stone!

So, here's how it works. You just list the names of the columns you want after the SELECT keyword, separated by commas. For instance, let's say you have a table called "customers" with columns like "id", "name", "email", and "phone_number". To retrieve only the "name" and "email" columns, you'd use this query:

```
SELECT name, email
FROM customers;
```

See? It's as simple as that. By explicitly stating which columns you want, you can narrow down your focus to the important stuff and make your queries more efficient. No more wasting time sifting through a sea of unnecessary data.

But wait, there's more! What if you want to display the retrieved data with different column names or do some calculations on the values? Well, that's where aliases come in. Aliases let you assign temporary names to columns or calculated values in the SELECT statement. It's like giving your data a makeover!

So, here's the drill. After the column name or calculation, you include the "AS" keyword followed by the alias name. Let's say you want to display the "name" column as "Customer Name" and calculate the total price of a product by multiplying its quantity and unit price. Here's how the query would look:

```
SELECT name AS "Customer Name", quantity * unit_price AS
"Total Price"
FROM orders;
```

By using aliases, you not only make your retrieved data easier to read but also give it some personality. I mean, who doesn't like a little flair, right?

But wait, there's more! Yes, you heard me right. There's more! You can also filter your data based on specific conditions. I know, mind-blowing stuff! By adding a WHERE clause to your query, you can narrow down your results to only the rows that meet those conditions. It's like having a secret weapon for precision!

So, here's how it works. The WHERE clause comes after the FROM clause and usually contains one or more conditions. A condition consists of a column, an operator, and a value. Let's say you only want to retrieve customers who made purchases in the year 2022. This is how the query would go:

```
SELECT *
FROM customers
WHERE year(purchase_date) = 2022;
```

In this query, we use the YEAR function to extract the year from the "purchase_date" column and compare it with the value 2022. Only the rows that fulfill this condition will be included in the result set. It's like magic!

Oh, but there's more! What if you want to combine multiple conditions? You can do that too! You can use logical operators like

AND and OR to create complex conditions. Let's say you want to retrieve customers who made purchases in 2022 and whose total purchase amount is greater than $100. Here's the query:

```
SELECT *
FROM customers
WHERE year(purchase_date) = 2022
AND total_purchase_amount > 100;
```

By filtering your data based on conditions, you can really narrow down your results to the most relevant information. It's like having a Sherlock Holmes-level of precision in your data analysis. It's amazing!

So, to sum it all up, we've covered a lot of ground in this chapter. We've learned how to retrieve specific columns, give them fancy names with aliases, and filter data based on conditions. The SELECT statement is the backbone of SQL data extraction, and by mastering its features, you can unleash the full potential of your database.

Filtering and Sorting Data

Ah, data retrieval. It's like trying to find a needle in a haystack, except the needle is the most relevant information and the haystack is a messy maze of data. But fear not, my fellow data adventurers, because SQL has got our backs. With a little bit of magic from WHERE clauses, comparison operators, and sorting techniques, we can turn that chaotic mess into a symphony of insights.

So, let's start with WHERE clauses. Think of them as our handy conductor, carefully selecting which instruments to bring in at a specific point in a symphony. In SQL, WHERE clauses allow us to set conditions for our data selection. We can filter out rows that don't meet our criteria, leaving us with a harmonious arrangement of information that fits our needs.

Let's paint a picture with an example. Imagine you're a retailer with a huge database of products, each with its own characteristics like price, brand, and availability. You want to find products within a certain price range, say between $50 and $100. With SQL, you can use a WHERE clause that says "price BETWEEN 50 AND 100." Boom. Only the products within that price range will make it onto your list.

But WHERE clauses aren't just for numerical values. Oh no, they can do so much more. Comparison operators, like "=", ">", "<", "<>", ">=", and "<=", are here to save the day. With these bad boys, we can compare values and retrieve rows that tick all our boxes. It's like finding the perfect pair of shoes that make your feet happy and your heart sing.

Here's another example to make things crystal clear. Imagine you're an HR manager with the task of finding employees whose salaries are above a certain threshold. In SQL, you can use the ">" operator to filter out the others. Just like that, your query "SELECT * FROM employees WHERE salary > 50000" will give you the exact subset of employees that meet your requirements.

Okay, now let's talk about sorting. Just like a composer arranging musical notes, we need to skillfully arrange our data to find valuable patterns. SQL gives us the magic of the ORDER BY clause to sort our data in ascending or descending order. It's like conducting an orchestra, guiding them from the softest to the loudest note.

To sort data in ascending order, we simply add "ORDER BY column_name ASC" to our query. For example, if we want to sort a list of products by price, we'd say "ORDER BY price ASC." It's like arranging them from the cheapest to the most expensive, creating a melodious sequence.

But wait, there's more! We can also sort data in descending order by using the keyword "DESC" instead of "ASC." So if we wanted to sort our products from most expensive to least expensive, we'd say "ORDER BY price DESC." It's like flipping the music sheet and unraveling a new layer of insights.

Whew, filtering and sorting data can be quite the adventure. It's like stepping into a symphony hall filled with possibilities. By refining our data retrieval process and perfectly sorting our data, we can uncover fascinating patterns and transform that raw data into a beautiful symphony of insights. So, let's keep playing those SQL notes, and strike the perfect chord of knowledge.

Filtering and sorting data are essential elements of the SQL Symphony. With WHERE clauses, comparison operators, and sorting techniques, we can extract the most relevant information from our vast datasets. It's like finding the shining stars in the night sky.

Joining Tables for Comprehensive Insights

As a seasoned data analyst and someone who has spent countless hours working with SQL, I can confidently say that table joins are like conducting a symphony. It's all about harmonizing different pieces of information to create a masterpiece of insights.

Table joins allow us to combine data from multiple sources and create a comprehensive dataset for further analysis. It's like stitching together a tapestry of information, bringing together different threads to create a coherent story.

So, let's start by laying the foundation and understanding the different types of table joins. We have the inner join, which is the simplest and most commonly used. This join only retains records that have matching values in both tables, filtering out the non-matching ones. It's perfect when we want to analyze data that exists in both tables at the same time.

Then we have the left join, which keeps all the records from the left table, regardless of whether there's a match in the right table. It's like keeping one foot in the comfort zone while exploring new territory. And of course, we also have the right join, which does the same, but with the roles of the left and right tables reversed.

These joins come in handy when we want to include all the data and still have the matching records.

But wait, there's more! We have the full outer join, which combines all the records from both tables, whether there's a match or not. It's like a grand reunion, bringing together all the available information into a single dataset. While this can result in a massive dataset, it opens up a world of possibilities for analyzing patterns and relationships that may have otherwise gone unnoticed.

The true power of table joins lies in their ability to uncover deeper insights by combining data from multiple tables. Take, for example, a retail business. By joining a table with customer information and another with purchase details, we can analyze individual buying habits, as well as broader trends like popular products, average spending per customer, and customer segmentation. It's like having a backstage pass to the inner workings of a business.

Table joins also allow us to perform complex calculations and aggregations on merged datasets. We can calculate total revenue by product, identify best-selling items, and analyze sales performance across different regions or time periods. It's like having a crystal ball that reveals the secrets of success.

But it doesn't stop there. Table joins also play a vital role in data cleansing and quality improvement. Sometimes, different sources of data may have inconsistencies or missing information. By merging these tables, we can uncover and correct any discrepancies. For example, by joining a table of customer addresses with a table of postal codes, we can ensure that all addresses are accurate and complete. It's like giving our data a makeover, making sure it's looking its best.

However, we must proceed with caution. Improper joins can lead to performance issues and impact the efficiency of our analysis, especially when dealing with large datasets. So, we need to optimize our join queries, use appropriate indexing, and make sure our join conditions are based on indexed columns whenever possible. It's like fine-tuning an instrument, ensuring that every note is played perfectly.

In addition to understanding the different types of joins, we need to grasp the concept of join conditions. These conditions specify the criteria for combining rows from different tables. They can be simple, involving just one column from each table, or more complex, involving multiple columns or logical operations. It's like solving a puzzle, fitting the pieces together to create a complete picture.

When defining join conditions, we must also consider the relationships between tables. In SQL, these relationships are established using primary keys and foreign keys. The primary key uniquely identifies each record in a table, while the foreign key refers to the primary key of another table. By leveraging these relationships, we can determine the appropriate columns to join on and ensure the accuracy and meaning of our merged dataset. It's like following a map, finding our way through the maze of data.

Here are some examples of SQL queries to illustrate different types of joins in the context of a hypothetical database with two tables: "Customers" and "Orders." These tables are commonly used for explaining SQL joins:

1. Inner Join:

An inner join returns only the rows that have matching values in both tables.

Example:

```
```
SELECT Customers.CustomerName, Orders.OrderID
FROM Customers
INNER JOIN Orders ON Customers.CustomerID = Orders.CustomerID;
```
```

2.   *Left Join (or Left Outer Join):*

A left join returns all rows from the left table and the matched rows from the right table. If there are no matches, NULL values are returned for the right table.

Example:

```
```
SELECT Customers.CustomerName, Orders.OrderID
FROM Customers
LEFT JOIN Orders ON Customers.CustomerID = Orders.CustomerID;
```
```

3.   *Right Join (or Right Outer Join):*

A right join returns all rows from the right table and the matched rows from the left table. If there are no matches, NULL values are returned for the left table.

Example:

```
```
SELECT Customers.CustomerName, Orders.OrderID
FROM Customers
RIGHT JOIN Orders ON Customers.CustomerID = Orders.CustomerID;
```
```

4.   *Full Outer Join (or Full Join):*

A full outer join returns all rows when there is a match in either the left or right table. If there are no matches, NULL values are returned for the table without a match.

Example:

```
```
SELECT Customers.CustomerName, Orders.OrderID
FROM Customers
```
```

```
    FULL  JOIN  Orders  ON  Customers.CustomerID  =
Orders.CustomerID;
```

These examples demonstrate how SQL joins can be used to combine data from two or more tables based on a common column. The type of join used determines which rows are included in the result set.

In conclusion, understanding the power of table joins is essential for comprehensive data analysis. It opens up a world of possibilities for uncovering insights, enhancing data quality, and conducting complex calculations. It's like conducting a symphony, bringing together different instruments to create a harmonious masterpiece. So, let's embrace the symphony of table joins and unlock the full potential of our data analytics endeavors.

CHAPTER 4

SQL RYTHM – DATA TRANSFORMATION

Modifying Data With UPDATE and DELETE

So, let me tell you about this whole SQL thing I've been getting into lately. It's pretty mind-blowing how powerful it is. I mean, not only can it fetch and manipulate data, but it can also modify and update it! And that's where the real heroes, the UPDATE and DELETE statements, come into play.

The UPDATE statement is like my trusty tool for tweaking existing data in a table. It's like magic, really. With just a few clicks and taps, I can change names, update contact info, or fix errors. It's all about maintaining the integrity of the database while keeping things up-to-date.

So, here's how it works. First, I have to figure out which table and column I want to modify. Once I've got that figured out, I just craft the statement accordingly. It's a pretty straightforward process, really. I start with the keyword "UPDATE," followed by the name of the table. Then comes the magic keyword "SET," which lets me specify the column and its new value. And finally, there's this thing called the "WHERE" clause that helps me define the conditions for the updates.

Let's say I have this table called "Employees." It's got columns like "FirstName," "LastName," and "Department." Now, imagine I want to change the department of an employee with the last name

"Smith" to "Marketing." Easy peasy! I just write the UPDATE statement like this:

```
UPDATE Employees
SET Department = 'Marketing'
WHERE LastName = 'Smith';
```

And just like that, the employee's department gets updated smoothly, syncing their data with the rest of the gang. It's incredible how SQL lets me modify data with such speed and accuracy.

But here's the exciting part. The more I dive into the UPDATE statement, the more complex scenarios I come across. Sometimes, I need to modify multiple columns in a single statement. Other times, I have to update rows based on multiple conditions. And you know what? SQL's got my back. It empowers me to handle these situations effortlessly, like I'm some sort of data modification maestro.

Let me give you another example. Let's imagine I need to update an employee's salary and job title based on their performance rating. No problem! The UPDATE statement can handle it. I just write it like this:

```
UPDATE Employees
SET Salary = Salary * 1.1, JobTitle = 'Senior Analyst'
WHERE PerformanceRating > 4;
```

Boom! Not only does the statement increase the employee's salary by 10%, but it also promotes them to the position of a Senior Analyst. It's like orchestrating the perfect symphony of data modification.

Now, while the UPDATE statement gives me the power to modify data, it's also important to recognize the significance of the

DELETE statement. This bad boy allows me to remove specific rows from a table, which comes in handy when I need to get rid of data that's no longer needed or relevant.

But hold your horses! Deletion is serious business. I have to be careful and really think it through because once the data's gone, it's gone for good. No take-backsies here. So, before I hit that delete button, I make sure to evaluate the consequences and make damn sure I'm not deleting something valuable by accident. It's all about being meticulous and precise.

So, how does the DELETE statement work? It's pretty straightforward too. I start with the keyword "DELETE FROM," followed by the table name. Then, I throw in a "WHERE" clause to define the condition for deletion. Let's say I want to remove all the employees from the "Sales" department. Simple! Here's the DELETE statement:

```
DELETE FROM Employees
WHERE Department = 'Sales';
```

And just like that, all rows in the "Employees" table that belong to the "Sales" department disappear into thin air. But let me tell you, I've got to be extra cautious here. I have to ensure that my actions align with the organization's goals. Data integrity is vital, and I take that responsibility seriously.

But here's the thing, while the DELETE statement is a potent tool for managing data, there are alternative approaches I can consider. SQL has these mechanisms like soft deletion or archiving that let me preserve data history and retain valuable information, even if it's no longer actively used.

As I take a step back and think about my journey with the UPDATE and DELETE statements, I can't help but be in awe of their role in the world of data analytics. These statements give me the power to modify and update existing data effortlessly, ensuring its accuracy, relevance, and integrity. It's like conducting an orchestra, using SQL as my harmonious instrument to create a masterpiece of data analytics. Pretty cool, huh?

Creating New Tables With CREATE

Alright, folks, let's dive into the fascinating world of SQL database creation! Now, before we can start building our shiny new tables, it's important to understand the ins and outs of the CREATE statement. This powerful statement is the key to creating all sorts of database objects like tables, indexes, views, and procedures. But for now, let's focus on tables, shall we?

So, here's how the CREATE statement works. It's simple, really. It starts with the keyword "CREATE," followed by the object type (which in our case is "TABLE"), and then the table name. Alright, imagine we want to create a table to store data about our customers. We can call it "Customers." So, the beginning of our CREATE statement would be "CREATE TABLE Customers." Sounds easy enough, right?

Now, onto Step 2: defining our table's columns and data types. Columns are the individual bits of information that our table will hold. Each column has a name and a data type, which determines the kind of data it can accept.

Let's transport ourselves into a customer-centric dream for a moment. Our imaginary Customers table should have columns for customer ID, name, email address, and date of birth. To define these columns within our CREATE statement, we use parentheses after the table name and separate each column definition with a trusty comma. So, to define the column name and data type, we use the syntax "column_name data_type."

Here's what our CREATE statement would look like for the Customers table:

```
CREATE TABLE Customers (
  customer_id INT,
```

```
   name VARCHAR(50),
   email VARCHAR(100),
   date_of_birth DATE
);
```

In this example, we've defined our chummy columns. We've got the "customer_id" column with a data type of INT (which is just a fancy name for integers), "name" with a data type of VARCHAR (that's "variable character" for you) and a maximum length of 50 characters, "email" with a data type of VARCHAR and a maximum length of 100 characters, and finally, "date_of_birth" with a data type of DATE. Beautiful, just beautiful.

Primary Keys

Now, onto Step 3: establishing some juicy relationships between our tables. In the magical world of relational databases, data is often spread across multiple tables that are linked together through captivating relationships. These relationships help us organize and manage data in the most efficient way possible. And to create these relationships, we rely on primary and foreign keys.

A primary key acts as a unique identifier for each record in a table. It ensures that every record stands out and has its own identity. In our Customers table, the customer ID is a prime candidate to serve as the primary key.

To designate a primary key column, we simply add the "PRIMARY KEY" constraint after its definition. Let's spruce up our CREATE statement and add that primary key, shall we?

```
CREATE TABLE Customers (
   customer_id INT PRIMARY KEY,
   name VARCHAR(50),
   email VARCHAR(100),
   date_of_birth DATE
);
```

Bravo! Our Customers table now has a shining primary key.

Foreign Keys

But wait, there's more! We also have foreign keys to consider. A foreign key is a reference to the primary key in another table. It's like a secret pathway that connects two tables, allowing us to fetch related data with ease. Let's say we have an Orders table that records customer orders. We can create a connection between the Customers and Orders tables by adding a foreign key column to the Orders table, which references the primary key column in the Customers table.

Let's take a look at the modified CREATE statement for our Orders table:

```
CREATE TABLE Orders (
  order_id INT PRIMARY KEY,
  customer_id INT,
  order_date DATE,
  FOREIGN KEY (customer_id) REFERENCES Customers(customer_id)
);
```

In this revised masterpiece, we've added a cool new column called "customer_id" to the Orders table, which will serve as our smooth foreign key. The "FOREIGN KEY" constraint is used to let the database know that "customer_id" is indeed a foreign key, and it points to the primary key column ("customer_id") in the Customers table.

Now, buckle up, because we're about to soar into Step 4: executing the CREATE statement. After defining our columns, data types, and establishing those thrilling relationships, it's time to make magic happen. We can execute the CREATE statement using a SQL command-line interface like MySQL or a software application that supports SQL.

Once the CREATE statement is successfully executed, our new table will come to life, ready to be filled with glorious data.

Therefore, creating tables with the CREATE statement is a vital step in the grand scheme of organizing and storing your precious data. Armed with a crystal-clear understanding of the syntax, column definitions, and relationships, we can create tables that will perfectly suit our data analysis needs.

Refining Data With ALTER

Let me tell you about the ALTER statement in SQL. It's like a magician's wand for data analysts, giving us the power to modify the structure of existing database objects and shape our data to fit our evolving needs. I've been working with SQL for quite some time now, and let me tell you, I've become quite skilled in using the ALTER statement to refine and optimize data.

One of the coolest things you can do with the ALTER statement is adding and modifying columns. Columns are the building blocks of a table, and they determine what type of data can be stored in each field. By adding new columns or tweaking existing ones, we can make our data more flexible and user-friendly.

So, let's say you have a table with customer information, and you need to add a new column to store email addresses. You've got to choose the right data type for the column and make sure it can handle all those email addresses. You can even throw in some constraints to enforce data integrity, like unique values or making sure the field can't be left blank.

But it's not just about adding columns. The ALTER statement also lets you modify existing columns. Imagine you have a column that's storing dates as character strings. That's not very helpful when you want to do date-specific analysis. So, with the ALTER statement, you can change the data type of the column to the appropriate one for dates. Boom, data consistency and date functions at your fingertips.

But here's the juicy part - the ALTER statement isn't just for making structural changes to tables. You can also use it to refine the data itself. Talk about a double whammy! With operations like inserting, updating, and deleting records, you can fix data anomalies and filter out any irrelevant or erroneous data.

So, let's say you have a table with customer data, but some of the rows are missing demographic information. No worries! You can use the INSERT operation to add new records and fill in those gaps. Suddenly, you have a more complete dataset ready for analysis.

And if you find a mistake in the data, like a customer changing their address, you can use the magical UPDATE statement to make the necessary adjustments. Keeping the data accurate and up to date is crucial for smooth analysis with no hiccups.

Now, for the grand finale, we have the DELETE statement. It's like the master of eliminating unnecessary entries. Whenever you encounter duplicates or obsolete records, you can use the DELETE statement to make them disappear, leaving behind a mighty, accurate dataset ready for analysis.

But hold your horses! While the ALTER statement is a powerful tool, you can't just go waving it around without caution. Any changes you make to the data carry the risk of introducing errors or compromising its integrity. You've got to know your data structure inside out and understand the consequences of your actions before you hit that execute button. Backing up your data or working in a controlled testing environment can also save you from any unwanted surprises.

So, in a nutshell, the ALTER statement is like the conductor's baton of data refining in SQL. By adding and modifying columns, we can fine-tune our data structure to extract accurate insights. And with operations like inserting, updating, and deleting records, we can make sure our dataset is primed and ready for analysis. But always remember to approach data refining with caution and precision to avoid any unforeseen mishaps. With the ALTER statement in your toolkit and a deep understanding of its tricks and techniques, you'll be orchestrating beautiful melodies of data analytics in no time.

SQL for Data Transformation Scenario in Data Analytics

To wrap up on using SQL for data transformation, here's a real-world data analysis scenario that demonstrates the use of SQL for transforming data:

Scenario: Customer Segmentation for a Retail Business

In this scenario, you're working for a retail business that wants to gain a better understanding of its customer base and tailor its marketing strategies accordingly. The goal is to segment customers into different groups based on their purchase behavior and demographics.

Data Preparation:

- Data Collection:

  The first step is to collect data from various sources, including sales records, customer profiles, and transaction history.

- Data Cleaning:

  The data may contain inconsistencies, missing values, or duplicates. You can use SQL to clean the data by removing duplicates, filling in missing values, and ensuring data consistency.

- Data Transformation with SQL:
  - Creating Customer Segments:

    To segment customers, you can use SQL to analyze their purchase history. For example, you may want to categorize customers as "Frequent Shoppers," "Occasional Shoppers," or "One-time Shoppers" based on the number and value of their purchases.

```
```
SELECT
  CustomerID,
  CASE
    WHEN TotalPurchaseAmount >= 1000
THEN 'Frequent Shopper'
    WHEN TotalPurchaseAmount >= 100
THEN 'Occasional Shopper'
    ELSE 'One-time Shopper'
  END AS CustomerSegment
FROM
  CustomerPurchases;
```
```

- o Demographic Segmentation:

  In addition to purchase behavior, you can also use SQL to segment customers by demographics. For example, you can categorize them by age groups, locations, or gender.

```
```
SELECT
  CustomerID,
  CASE
    WHEN Age < 25 THEN 'Young Adults'
    WHEN Age >= 25 AND Age < 40 THEN
'Middle-aged'
    ELSE 'Seniors'
  END AS AgeGroup
FROM
  CustomerProfiles;
```
```

- o Combining Segments:

  You can further use SQL to combine the purchase behavior and demographic segments to create a comprehensive customer segmentation model.

```
```
SELECT
    CustomerID,
    PurchaseSegment,
    DemographicSegment
FROM
    CustomerPurchases
JOIN
        CustomerDemographics
ON
        CustomerPurchases.CustomerID   =
CustomerDemographics.CustomerID;
```
```

- Analysis and Decision-Making:
  - o Analysis:

    Once you have created customer segments, you can analyze the behavior of each group. For example, you might find that "Frequent Shoppers" tend to respond well to certain promotions, while "Occasional Shoppers" prefer different incentives.

  - o Tailored Marketing:

    With the insights gained from SQL-based data transformation, you can tailor marketing campaigns to target each customer segment more effectively. For instance, you can send personalized offers to "One-time Shoppers" to encourage repeat purchases.

By using SQL for data transformation, we've successfully turned raw data into actionable insights that help the retail business understand its customers better and make data-driven decisions to improve its marketing strategies and customer experience.

CHAPTER 5

SQL INTERMEZZO - DATA ANALYSIS

Aggregating Data With GROUP BY

Alright folks, buckle up because we're about to dive into the wild world of SQL and the mystical realm of the GROUP BY clause. Let's break down the process step-by-step, complete with practical examples and explanations. By the time we're done here, you'll be wielding the power to tame your unruly data and unlock its true analytical potential.

But before we jump straight into the nitty-gritty of the GROUP BY clause, let's take a moment to get on the same page about what aggregation really means. When we talk about aggregating data, we're talking about summarizing or combining multiple rows of data into a single value. It's like squeezing a bunch of information into a nice, neat package, making it easier to spot patterns and extract insights.

This is where the GROUP BY clause swoops in to save the day. Think of it as a majestic gateway that allows us to categorize our data based on common attributes and then perform wicked cool aggregate functions on each group. These functions, like SUM, COUNT, AVG, MIN, and MAX, give us the power to perform calculations on our grouped data, and boy, do they spit out some tasty metrics.

To really grasp the power of the GROUP BY clause, let's jump into a hypothetical scenario. Picture this: you work for a booming e-commerce company and you've got a beastly dataset that's chock full of customer information. You've got their names, the amounts they've spent, purchase dates, and even where they're located. Now, by using the GROUP BY clause, you can group the data based on location and then apply those wicked aggregate functions to calculate some sweet metrics like total revenue generated from each location or the average purchase amount per location.

With me so far? Great, let's break it down step-by-step.

Step 1: Identify the Columns for Grouping

First things first, you got to figure out which columns you want to use as the basis for grouping. These columns should be shared attributes among the rows you want to aggregate. In our e-commerce scenario, we'd choose the "location" column as our knight in shining armor.

Step 2: Define the GROUP BY Clause in the SQL Query

Once you've got your columns for grouping, it's time to bring in the big guns. Incorporate the GROUP BY clause into your SQL query, right after the WHERE clause and before the ORDER BY clause if you're feeling fancy.

No need to stress about the syntax, it's a piece of cake. Just list out the columns you want to group by, separated by commas. In our scenario, it would look a little something like this:

```
GROUP BY location
```

Step 3: Apply Aggregate Functions to the Grouped Data

Alright, hold on to your hats because now it's time to unleash those legendary aggregate functions on your grouped data. These functions will work their magic, performing calculations within each group to give you some seriously juicy metrics.

There's a whole arsenal of aggregate functions at your disposal, but let's focus on a few of the heavy hitters:

1. *SUM:* This bad boy calculates the total sum of a numeric column for each group. So, in our e-commerce extravaganza, we could use it to figure out the total revenue generated from each location.
2. *COUNT:* The COUNT function does exactly what it says - it counts the number of rows in each group. Super useful for tallying up how many customers we have in each location.
3. *AVG:* The AVG function calculates the average value of a numeric column for each group. So, we could use it to find the average purchase amount for each location.
4. *MIN:* This sneaky function snatches the minimum value from a numeric column within each group. Great for sniffing out the lowest purchase amount in each location.
5. *MAX:* Now the MAX function loves to show off by grabbing the maximum value from a numeric column within each group. It'll help us spot the highest purchase amount for each location.

To put these functions to use, just slide them right into your SQL query like a well-oiled machine. For example, if we wanted to calculate the total revenue and average purchase amount for each location, our query might look something like this:

```
```
SELECT location, SUM(purchase_amount) AS total_revenue,
    AVG(purchase_amount) AS average_purchase_amount
FROM customers
GROUP BY location;
```
```

Step 4: Customize the Output with ORDER BY and HAVING Clauses

Now that you've applied those mighty aggregate functions, you might want to spruce up the output of your query. Lucky for you, we've got two extra clauses up our sleeves: ORDER BY and HAVING.

The ORDER BY clause lets you sort the results based on specified columns. In our magical e-commerce land, we might want to sort the locations in descending order of total revenue. So, we'd just add this line to our query:

```
ORDER BY total_revenue DESC
```

On the other hand, the HAVING clause gives you the power to filter the grouped data based on specific conditions. Let's say we only want to include locations with a total revenue greater than a certain threshold. You guessed it, we'd add the HAVING clause like this:

```
HAVING total_revenue > 10000
```

These extra clauses bring a whole lot of pizzazz and allow you to fine-tune your analysis to fit your needs.

Step 5: Execute the Query and Analyze the Results

Alright, it's showtime! Once you've got your SQL query all spruced up with the GROUP BY clause, aggregate functions, and any extra flair, it's time to hit that execute button and see what your data reveals. Take a good look at the grouped and summarized data, paying close attention to those delicious metrics produced by the aggregate functions. These insights will guide your decision-making process and lay the foundation for some savvy business moves.

To wrap it all up, understanding how to befriend the GROUP BY clause in SQL is crucial for any data analyst or decision-making whiz. It lets us mold our unruly data into something we can actually work with, extracting insights and spotting patterns that would have otherwise stayed hidden. Those aggregate functions are like a caped superhero, giving us the power to perform some seriously cool calculations and generate meaningful metrics.

We've explored the step-by-step process of using the GROUP BY clause, from picking the columns for grouping all the way to customizing the output. By weaving the GROUP BY clause into our SQL queries, we can harmonize our data and unleash its analytical potential.

So armed with the knowledge of the GROUP BY clause, you're ready to navigate the vast ocean of data. Go forth and unlock the symphony of insights hidden within, delivering harmonious data analytics that'll make the world go wild.

Calculations and Functions in SQL

I can't help but be captivated by the symphony that is SQL. It's like diving into a world of possibilities, where mathematical operations dance gracefully with numeric data. SQL offers an array of mathematical functions that add, subtract, multiply, and divide, allowing us to mold our data into a masterpiece of insights. Like a skilled conductor, we can use these functions to calculate the total revenue generated by a company or the average customer rating for a product.

But SQL doesn't stop there. It's got a whole repertoire of advanced mathematical functions that can send shivers down your spine. Take the exponentiation function, for example. It's like the maestro of compound interest and growth rates, bringing precision and complexity to our calculations. And let's not forget about the logarithmic function, a powerful tool for financial analysis and tackling exponential growth or decay.

CONCAT And SUBSTRING Functions

Now, let's turn our attention to the dancers of SQL - the string manipulation functions. They bring life and meaning to our text data, allowing us to slice and dice it with finesse. The CONCAT function is like a master of synchronization, seamlessly putting together different strings to create a comprehensive description or report. And the SUBSTRING function? It's our partner in crime when we only need a specific segment of a vast sea of text, like addresses or descriptions.

Using CONCAT Function:

You're working with a database that stores customer names, and you want to create a report that combines the first name and last name into a single full name.

```
SELECT CONCAT(FirstName, ' ', LastName) AS FullName
FROM Customers;
```

In this example, the `CONCAT` function is used to combine the "FirstName" and "LastName" columns, separated by a space, into a new column named "FullName." The result will provide you with the full names of customers.

Also, assume your database contains a "Product" table, and you need to generate product codes by concatenating the product category and product ID.

```
SELECT CONCAT(Category, '-', ProductID) AS ProductCode
FROM Products;
```

Here, the `CONCAT` function is used to combine the "Category" and "ProductID" columns with a hyphen, creating a new column called "ProductCode" containing the product codes.

Using SUBSTRING Function:

You have a database that stores product descriptions, and you want to extract the first 50 characters of each description for a summary.

```
SELECT SUBSTRING(Description, 1, 50) AS ShortDescription
FROM Products;
```

The `SUBSTRING` function is used here to retrieve the first 50 characters from the "Description" column, creating a new column named "ShortDescription" that contains the abbreviated product descriptions.

Again, your database stores email addresses, and you want to extract the domain names (everything after the "@" symbol).

```
SELECT SUBSTRING(Email, CHARINDEX('@', Email) + 1,
LEN(Email) - CHARINDEX('@', Email)) AS Domain
FROM Customers;
```

In this example, the `SUBSTRING` function, along with `CHARINDEX` and `LEN`, is used to extract the domain part of email addresses. The result is stored in a new column called "Domain."

TIMESTAMP And DATEADD Functions

Ah, but we can't overlook the importance of date and time in our data analysis. SQL has us covered there too, with functions that can bend time to our will. The TIMESTAMP function adds a touch of magic, allowing us to extract the year, month, or day from a timestamp or calculate the difference between two timestamps. And the DATEADD function, oh boy, it's like a time traveler, armed with the ability to add or subtract days, months, or years from a given date. Perfect for analyzing trends over time or calculating durations.

Using TIMESTAMP Function:

You have a database that stores order timestamps, and you want to extract the year and month to analyze monthly sales trends.

```
SELECT
  ORDER_ID,
  EXTRACT(YEAR FROM OrderTimestamp) AS OrderYear,
  EXTRACT(MONTH FROM OrderTimestamp) AS OrderMonth
FROM Orders;
```

In this example, the `TIMESTAMP` function is used to extract the year and month from the "OrderTimestamp" column. The results are stored in new columns "OrderYear" and "OrderMonth," allowing you to analyze sales data by year and month.

If your database contains employee records with hire dates, and you want to calculate the duration of their employment in years.

```
SELECT
  EmployeeID,
  DATE_DIFF(CURRENT_DATE(), HireDate, YEAR) AS YearsEmployed
FROM Employees;
```

Here, the `TIMESTAMP` function and `DATE_DIFF` function are used to calculate the number of years an employee has been employed. The result is stored in a column named "YearsEmployed."

Using DATEADD Function:

You're working with a database that stores subscription start dates, and you want to calculate the end date by adding three months to each start date.

```
```
SELECT
    SubscriptionID,
    StartDate,
    DATEADD(MONTH, 3, StartDate) AS EndDate
FROM Subscriptions;
```
```

The `DATEADD` function is used here to add three months to each "StartDate" and calculate the "EndDate." This is useful for managing subscription periods.

Also, you have a database with event dates, and you want to find the date six months in the future for each event.

```
```
SELECT
    EventID,
    EventDate,
    DATEADD(MONTH, 6, EventDate) AS FutureDate
FROM Events;
```
```

In this case, the `DATEADD` function is used to calculate a date six months in the future for each event's "EventDate." The results are stored in a column named "FutureDate."

These examples demonstrate how the TIMESTAMP function can extract specific components of date and time, while the DATEADD function can manipulate dates and times by adding or subtracting units like days, months, or years. These functions are valuable for time-based data analysis in SQL.

COUNT, SUM, AVG, MIN, and MAX Functions

But what about the ensemble? The aggregate functions that lead the data analysis orchestra. COUNT, SUM, AVG, MIN, and MAX. They work harmoniously to summarize and analyze data across multiple rows. COUNT helps us count the rows in a table or the occurrences of a specific value. SUM lets us calculate the total sum of a numeric column, while AVG gives us the average value. And MIN and MAX? They find the lowest and highest values in a column, like the stars of the show.

Consider a situation where you have a sales database with order data, and you want to analyze the total number of orders, the sum of order amounts, the average order amount, and find the minimum and maximum order amounts.

```
SELECT
    COUNT(*) AS TotalOrders,
    SUM(OrderAmount) AS TotalOrderAmount,
    AVG(OrderAmount) AS AverageOrderAmount,
    MIN(OrderAmount) AS MinOrderAmount,
    MAX(OrderAmount) AS MaxOrderAmount
FROM Orders;
```

In this query, we used the following aggregate functions:

- `COUNT(*)` counts the total number of rows in the "Orders" table, giving us the "TotalOrders."
- `SUM(OrderAmount)` calculates the sum of the "OrderAmount" column, providing the "TotalOrderAmount."

- `AVG(OrderAmount)` computes the average of the "OrderAmount" column, giving us the "AverageOrderAmount."
- `MIN(OrderAmount)` finds the minimum value in the "OrderAmount" column, resulting in the "MinOrderAmount."
- `MAX(OrderAmount)` identifies the maximum value in the "OrderAmount" column, giving us the "MaxOrderAmount."

This single SQL query provides a comprehensive summary of order data, showing the total number of orders, the sum of order amounts, the average order amount, and the minimum and maximum order amounts in one go.

The CASE Statement

We can't forget about conditional calculations either. SQL has a trick up its sleeve for that too - the CASE statement. With this powerful tool, we can perform different calculations based on specific conditions. It's like having a magician by our side, helping us calculate discounts based on customer loyalty or categorizing data into different groups based on specific criteria.

The `CASE` statement in SQL is a versatile tool for performing conditional calculations and data categorization. Here's an example of how you can use it:

If you have a customer database, and you want to categorize customers into loyalty tiers based on their purchase history. You'll use the `CASE` statement to determine which tier each customer belongs to.

```
```
SELECT
    CustomerName,
    TotalPurchases,
    CASE
```
```

```
      WHEN TotalPurchases >= 1000 THEN 'Gold'
      WHEN TotalPurchases >= 500 THEN 'Silver'
      ELSE 'Bronze'
   END AS LoyaltyTier
FROM Customers;
```

In this query, we're categorizing customers based on their "TotalPurchases." Here's how it works:

- If a customer's total purchases are greater than or equal to 1000, they are categorized as "Gold."
- If their total purchases are between 500 and 999, they are categorized as "Silver."
- If their total purchases are less than 500, they are categorized as "Bronze."

The `CASE` statement evaluates the conditions one by one and assigns the appropriate loyalty tier based on the customer's total purchases. This allows you to perform conditional calculations and categorize data effectively, making it a valuable tool in SQL for various scenarios.

User-Defined Functions

Let's not forget the user-defined functions, our loyal companions in this journey. These functions, created by us, for us, are like the soloists of the orchestra. They can be customized to meet our unique analysis needs, encapsulating complex calculations or repetitive tasks. With user-defined functions, SQL becomes even more versatile, enhancing the modularity and efficiency of our queries.

User-defined functions in SQL are indeed powerful tools that allow you to create custom functions tailored to your specific analysis needs. These functions can encapsulate complex calculations or repetitive tasks, enhancing the modularity and efficiency of your queries. Here's an example of how you can create and use a simple user-defined function in SQL:

Assuming you have a database with product prices, and you want to calculate the discounted price for each product using a custom discount function.

First, let's create a user-defined function that calculates the discounted price. We'll call it "CalculateDiscount."

```
CREATE FUNCTION CalculateDiscount(originalPrice DECIMAL, discountPercentage DECIMAL)
RETURNS DECIMAL
BEGIN
    DECLARE discountedPrice DECIMAL;
    SET discountedPrice = originalPrice - (originalPrice * (discountPercentage / 100));
    RETURN discountedPrice;
END;
```

This function takes two parameters: "originalPrice" and "discountPercentage." It calculates the discounted price and returns the result.

Now, you can use this user-defined function in your SQL queries to calculate discounted prices:

```
SELECT
    ProductName,
    Price,
    CalculateDiscount(Price, 10) AS DiscountedPrice
FROM Products;
```

In this query, we select the product name, the original price, and use the "CalculateDiscount" function to calculate the discounted price with a 10% discount. The user-defined function streamlines the calculation and allows you to reuse it in various queries.

User-defined functions in SQL provide flexibility and modularity, making your queries more efficient and your database more manageable. They are like soloists in the orchestra, adding unique capabilities to your SQL toolkit.

As I immerse myself in this symphony of calculations, I am constantly in awe of the power and flexibility of SQL. It's like a magician's hat, hiding endless possibilities to transform raw data into valuable insights. Whether it's playing with basic mathematical operations, dancing with strings, or bending time, SQL gives us the tools to create our own masterpiece of harmonized, manipulated data.

Crafting Subqueries for Advanced Analysis

Alright, before we dive into the practical applications and techniques of using subqueries in SQL, let's make sure we're all on the same page. So, what exactly is a subquery? Well, it's basically a fancy term for a query within another query, enclosed within parentheses. You can put a subquery inside a SELECT, INSERT, UPDATE, or DELETE statement. The interesting thing about subqueries is that they can retrieve data from one or multiple tables, and the result of the subquery can be used in various ways by the outer query.

Now, let's take it a step further and talk about nested subqueries. These are subqueries that are nested within each other, like Russian nesting dolls. This allows us to build really complex queries by nesting multiple subqueries within one another. The result of the innermost subquery is used by the outer subquery, and that result is then used by the outermost query. It's like a chain reaction of subqueries, enabling us to perform advanced analysis and get results that would be almost impossible to achieve with just a single query.

On the flip side, we have correlated subqueries. These are subqueries that actually refer to a column from the outer query. Each row of the outer query triggers the evaluation of the subquery, and the result of that subquery is based on the current row being processed. The correlation between the subquery and the outer query allows us to perform some seriously sophisticated analysis that requires data from both the outer query and the subquery.

Why Subqueries?

Now that we have the basics down, let's talk about why subqueries are so useful. One of the most common use cases for subqueries is filtering and sorting data. With a subquery, we can retrieve a specific subset of data that meets certain criteria. Let me give you an example. Imagine we have a database of customers, and we want to find all the customers who have made a purchase in the past month. We can do this by using a subquery to select the customer IDs from the orders table, and then using this subquery as a filter in the main query to retrieve the customer details.

Here's an example SQL query to illustrate it:

```
```
SELECT *
FROM customers
WHERE customer_id IN
(
    SELECT customer_id FROM orders
    WHERE order_date >= DATE_SUB(
        NOW(), INTERVAL 1 MONTH
)
);
```
```

In this example, the subquery `(SELECT customer_id FROM orders WHERE order_date >= DATE_SUB(NOW(), INTERVAL 1 MONTH))` retrieves the customer IDs of those who have made a purchase in the past month. The main query then uses the `IN` operator to filter the customers based on these IDs.

But wait, there's more! Nested subqueries take subqueries to a whole new level. By nesting multiple subqueries, we can perform even more complex analysis and derive powerful insights from our data. Let's consider another scenario - we have a database of products, and we want to find the customers who have purchased the most expensive product in each category. To achieve this, we can use nested subqueries to determine the maximum price for each category, and then use these subqueries to filter and retrieve the corresponding customer details.

Here's an example SQL query to show you what I mean:

```
SELECT *
FROM customers
WHERE customer_id IN (
  SELECT customer_id
  FROM orders
  WHERE product_id IN (
    SELECT product_id
    FROM products
    WHERE price = (SELECT MAX(price) FROM products WHERE category = 'Electronics')
  )
);
```

In this example, the nested subquery `(SELECT MAX(price) FROM products WHERE category = 'Electronics')` retrieves the maximum price for the 'Electronics' category. This subquery is then used in another subquery to filter the product IDs for that category. Finally, the outermost query uses this nested subquery to filter the customer IDs based on the purchased products.

Correlated Subqueries

Now, let's talk about correlated subqueries. These babies take our data analysis capabilities to a whole new level of sophistication. By establishing a connection between the subquery and the outer query, we can perform analysis that requires data from both sources.

Let's explore a scenario where we have a database of employees, and we want to find the average salary of employees in each department, along with the number of employees who earn more than the average salary of their department. We can do this by using a correlated subquery to calculate the average salary for each department and then comparing each employee's salary to this average within the subquery.

Check out this example SQL query to see it in action:

```
```
SELECT department_id, AVG(salary) AS average_salary,
 (SELECT COUNT(employee_id)
  FROM employees AS e2
  WHERE e1.department_id = e2.department_id
  AND e2.salary > (SELECT AVG(salary)
          FROM employees
          WHERE department_id = e1.department_id)
) AS num_employees_above_avg
FROM employees AS e1
GROUP BY department_id;
```
```

In this example, the outer query calculates the average salary for each department using the `AVG` function. The correlated subquery then compares each employee's salary to this average within the subquery by selecting the count of employees who earn more than the average for their department. This count is then displayed in the main query as the `num_employees_above_avg` column.

In the world of data analysis, SQL is your trusty conductor, leading you through a symphony of possibilities. As you've seen, it offers a wide array of tools to harmonize, manipulate, and extract insights from your data. Whether you're dealing with numbers, strings, dates, or complex conditions, SQL empowers you to transform raw data into valuable insights. So, embrace these functions and clauses like the skilled instruments they are, and get ready to unlock the potential of your data. With SQL as your guide, you're well-equipped to navigate the vast ocean of information, creating harmonious data analytics that will set the stage for informed decisions and data-driven discoveries.

With a solid understanding of subqueries and their different forms, you now have a powerful tool in your hands for crafting advanced data analysis queries. By harnessing the power of nested and correlated subqueries, you can unlock all sorts of hidden insights within your data and tackle complex analysis scenarios with confidence. Don't forget to practice and experiment with these techniques to refine your skills and expand your analytical capabilities. As you continue your journey with SQL Symphony, get ready to unleash the symphony of harmonized data analytics at your command.

CHAPTER 6

SQL RECAPITULATION - DATA VISUALIZATION

Connecting SQL to Visualization Tools

Alright folks, let's dive right into this and talk about why connecting SQL to visualization tools is a game-changer. Picture this: you're trying to make sense of a mountain of data stored in those relational databases, and SQL, or Structured Query Language, is your secret weapon. It's the go-to programming language for data professionals like us, giving us the power to access, manipulate, and retrieve that precious information.

But hold on a second, how do we make all that data come to life? Well, that's where visualization tools swoop in. These tools let us transform that raw data into visually stunning charts, graphs, and dashboards that not only look super cool but also convey information like a boss.

Connecting SQL to visualization tools is like the perfect marriage of brains and beauty, helping us bridge the gap between raw data and impactful visualizations, and ultimately making our insights shine bright like diamonds.

Tableau

Okay, now let's get down to business and talk about the nitty-gritty of connecting SQL to these popular visualization tools. Brace yourselves, because we're about to embark on a thrilling step-by-step journey that'll make this connection a piece of cake.

Step 1: Choosing A Visualization Tool:

This is all about choosing your weapon of choice — the visualization tool. Now, there are more visualization tools out there than stars in the sky, each with its own unique set of features and fancy tricks. But today, my focus is on one of the heavyweights in the game: Tableau.

This tool right here is a powerhouse of data visualization, allowing us to create stunning visualizations and interactive dashboards without breaking a sweat. Tableau seamlessly integrates with SQL databases, making it the ultimate wingman for this whole connecting SQL to visualization extravaganza. So, if you're ready to roll with Tableau, buckle up and let's dive into the next step.

Step 2: Installing And Setting Up Tableau:

This brings us to the exhilarating task of installing and setting up Tableau. Trust me, it's simpler than you think.

Tableau Desktop:

First things first, you'll need to download and install this mighty tool called Tableau Desktop – this is where all the magic happens. Once it's up and running, you'll find yourself face to face with its user-friendly interface. On the left-hand side, there's this Connect pane waving at you like it knows the secret to your SQL dreams. Click on "To a Server" and select the SQL database you want to connect to. Think MySQL, PostgreSQL, or Microsoft SQL Server – take your pick.

Now, it's time to enter those oh-so-important connection details like server names, port numbers, database names, usernames, and passwords. Hit that "Connect" button, and just like that, Tableau will form a beautiful connection with your SQL database. It's like witnessing a cosmic connection happening right before your eyes.

Tableau Public:

Tableau Public is the go-to choice for those who prefer an online and user-friendly approach to data visualization. With Tableau Public, there's no need to worry about installation or setting up software on your local machine.

This web-based version of Tableau is connected to your SQL database the same way as the Desktop version. It lets you create, share, and explore interactive data visualizations right in your browser. All you need to do is visit the Tableau Public website, sign in or create an account, and you're ready to start building your visualizations.

It's a fantastic option for beginners and anyone who wants to quickly dive into the world of data visualization without the hassle of installation. Plus, it offers a convenient platform for sharing your insights with the world, making your data-driven storytelling accessible to a broader audience. So, whether you're an SQL enthusiast or just getting started, Tableau Public online brings data visualization within easy reach.

Step 3: Importing Data:

Now, let's move on to step 3, which involves importing data from your SQL database into Tableau. Hang on tight, folks, we're about to get some data action going. Tableau gives you a buffet of options for importing data – you can connect to individual tables, write some fancy SQL queries, or create your own custom SQL magic.

Want to connect to specific tables? Simply select them and click "Add" to bring them into your Tableau workspace. Feel like writing some SQL queries? Well, you're in luck because Tableau lets you do just that. You can retrieve specific data or perform wild transformations by writing SQL queries within Tableau itself. Once you've got that data just where you want it, Tableau will give you a little preview to make sure everything's A-OK. No surprises, just data goodness.

Step 4: Data Visualization:

My curious minds, is all about getting that data squeaky clean and ready for its close-up. Effective data visualization relies on data that's been buffed, polished, and treated like a VIP. Tableau's got your back here – with its drag-and-drop interface, you can easily filter, aggregate, join, and create calculated fields without getting tangled up in complicated coding.

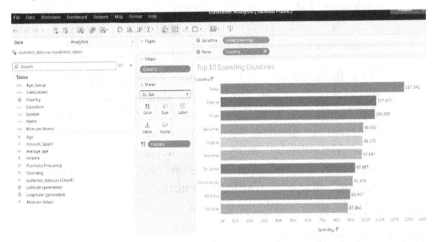

What's more, you can even define fancy relationships between tables to combine data from multiple sources. This is where you unlock the true power of your data, – by preparing and transforming it with Tableau, you uncover hidden gems and priceless insights that will send shockwaves through your decision-making process. Get busy with that data, people!

Step 5: Improve Your Visualization:

Okay, we're hurtling towards the finish line now with step 5. It's time to give your visuals some oomph! Tableau lets you work your magic and create eye-catching, jaw-dropping visualizations that'll make people drool.

You've got a treasure trove of options at your fingertips – bar charts, line charts, scatter plots, maps, and the list goes on. Want to create a beautiful bar chart? Just drag and drop the necessary fields onto the canvas, and voilà – Tableau will work its magic and whip up the perfect visualization for you. But hey, we're not done yet – you can customize those visualizations to your heart's content. Adjust colors, sizes, labels, and add interactivity to make your visualizations sing.

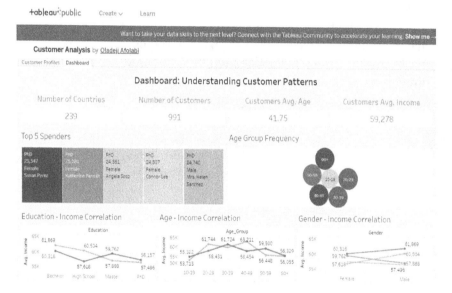

And if you're feeling adventurous, you can even create interactive dashboards by combining different visualizations, slapping on some filters and actions. It's like having your own data party right there on your screen. So go ahead, let your creativity run wild and make those visuals pop!

Step 6: Publish And Share Your Visualizations

Alright, we've reached the final step of this exhilarating journey – step 6! It's time to share your creations with the world. Tableau gives you the power to publish and share your visualizations in all kinds of ways. You've got Tableau Server, Tableau Public, and Tableau Online to choose from.

By publishing your visualizations, you're opening the gates and letting people from far and wide interact with your insights. Stakeholders and decision-makers will be walking through those gates, eager to explore that juicy data you've prepared.

And here's the cherry on top – you can even embed your Tableau visualizations in websites or share them via links or email. With Tableau, you're not just sharing insights – you're sharing a whole experience. Your data is about to go viral!

So, to wrap it all up, connecting SQL to visualization tools is like a match made in data heaven. By following these steps and mastering the art of this connection, you're unlocking a whole new dimension of data analysis and visual storytelling. Whether you're a data analyst, a business guru, or someone with dreams of conquering the data science world, this is your ticket to taking your insights to the next level. So grab some coffee, roll up those sleeves, and let's make sweet music with the symphony of SQL and visualization. Your data adventure awaits!

Creating Charts and Graphs

Alright, folks, let's dive into the wonderful world of charting! In this section, we're going to explore all sorts of chart types and techniques for creating visually stunning and informative charts and graphs using good old SQL data. We're going to take a deep dive into the fundamentals of charting, from figuring out which chart is best for your data to spicing up your charts to make them pop. So buckle up and get ready for a journey of harmonizing data and unleashing its true storytelling potential.

But wait, before we embark on this epic adventure, let's take a moment to appreciate just how important data visualization is. I mean, in today's data-driven world, being able to turn raw data into meaningful visual representations is like having a superpower. Data visualization is what helps us uncover patterns, identify correlations, track trends, and deliver insights that hit home. And charts and graphs, are like the superheroes of data visualization.

They make information come alive, making even the most complex datasets easier to understand and more engaging to digest.

Now, let's talk chart types. We've got a whole smorgasbord of options when it comes to creating charts using SQL data. Line charts, bar charts, pie charts, scatter plots, and area charts are just a few examples of the amazing array of chart types that SQL has in store for us.

Line Charts:

Line charts are like time travelers, perfect for tracking trends over time. They show data points connected by lines, allowing us to see how values change over a period.

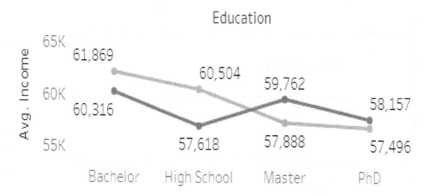

Say you want to showcase the sales growth of a hot product over a year - a line chart is your go-to chart type.

Bar Charts:

Now, let's head over to the land of bar charts. These are great at comparing quantities across different categories.

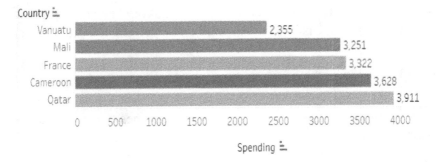

They come with vertical or horizontal bars that represent each category, and the length of the bar tells you the value you're measuring. So, if you want to compare revenue generated by different product categories in a specific quarter, a bar chart is your knight in shining armor.

Pie Charts:

Next up, we have pie charts.

These beauties are all about proportions and percentages. They represent data as slices of a circle, each slice representing a specific category or value. Think market share of different products in a specific market - that's where pie charts shine.

Scatter Plots:

Ah, scatter plots, the detectives of the charting world. These guys excel at identifying relationships and correlations between two variables.

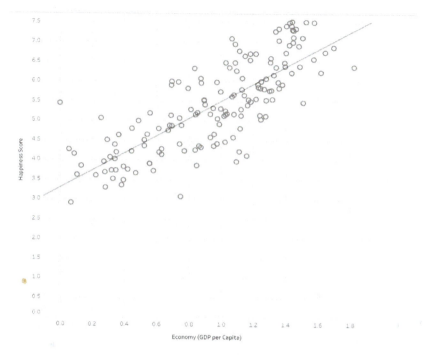

They show data as a bunch of points, with the position of each point revealing the relationship between the variables you're analyzing. So, if you want to investigate the connection between advertising expenditure and sales revenue, a scatter plot will help you crack the case.

Area Charts:

Last but not least, we've got area charts. These are like line charts on steroids - they emphasize accumulated values over time. They're like the architects of the chart world, displaying data as a series of filled areas stacked one on top of the other, representing the cumulative value at each point. Area charts are perfect for visualizing the growth of multiple variables over time, like tracking the market share of different competitors in a particular industry. Talk about versatile!

Visually Appealing Charts

Now that we've got a grasp on all these amazing chart types, let's turn our attention to creating visually appealing and informative charts and graphs using SQL data. One technique we need to master is the art of color, typography, and visual hierarchy.

Color, is your secret weapon in the world of charting. It brings life and excitement to your charts while helping you differentiate between categories and data points. When choosing colors, you got to make sure they're visually appealing and can effectively convey your message. If you're comparing revenue by product category in a particular quarter, why not sprinkle some different colors on each category to make the chart visually engaging and easier to understand?

Typography also plays a big role in the effectiveness of a chart. Choosing the right fonts, font sizes, and font weights can make your chart look professional and easy on the eyes. A bold font for the chart title and clear, legible fonts for axes labels...ah, now we're talking charting in style!

And let's not forget about *visual hierarchy*. It's all about arranging and emphasizing the visual elements in your chart. You can use visual cues like size, position, and color saturation to guide the viewer's attention and highlight the most important information. You want to make those crucial data points larger or more vibrant to draw attention and show their significance.

But *customization*, is where the real magic happens. Most charting tools give you a buffet of options to customize your charts. You can adjust axis labels, add legends or data labels, customize tooltips, and even whip up some fancy animations to enhance the user experience. Customization allows you to adapt the chart to your specific needs and make it visually appealing. Want to highlight a particular data point? Change its color or size. Need to emphasize certain categories? Play around with colors or patterns. The customization possibilities are endless!

SQL Queries Optimization

Now, hold on tight, because we've got one more thing to consider when creating charts and graphs using SQL data. And that's the underlying SQL queries and their performance. You see, as data analysts, we need to optimize our SQL queries to make sure we're fetching data efficiently, especially when we're dealing with colossal datasets. Proper indexing, filtering, and aggregation can significantly speed up query execution and make our charts and graphs perform like rock stars.

To wrap things up, creating visually appealing and informative charts and graphs using SQL data is an art form that combines charting techniques, data visualization principles, and SQL query optimization. By choosing the right chart type, harnessing the power of color, typography, and visual hierarchy, customizing your charts, and optimizing your SQL queries, you can unlock the true potential of your data and deliver invaluable insights to decision-makers.

Telling Data Stories With SQL-Driven Visuals

Join me on a journey as we dive into the world of SQL-driven visuals and discover how they can bring data stories to life.

Picture this: you have a wealth of raw data at your fingertips, but how do you make sense of it all and captivate your audience at the same time? That's where SQL-driven visuals swoop in like superheroes, transforming complex information into a concise and comprehensible format that can be understood by all.

First things first, let's appreciate the power of SQL-driven visuals. These babies have an uncanny knack for conveying information in a way that sticks with your audience. And by harnessing the might of SQL, we can not only extract and transform data but also present it in a visually captivating way, making those insights pop like fireworks on a summer night.

So, where do we begin? Step one is all about understanding the importance of SQL-driven visuals. We're not just dealing with pretty pictures here; we're talking about telling a story. And visuals are the key players in this game. They have the ability to simplify complex concepts and allow our audience to grasp the essence of the data with just one glance.

Step two is where the magic happens. We unearth the data we need and transform it using SQL. This process is like sculpting a masterpiece - we shape, mold, and refine the data until it portrays our story accurately. With SQL's powerful tools, we can dig into databases, merge tables, and apply filters to extract the juiciest nuggets of information. It's like being a detective piecing together clues to unravel a thrilling mystery.

Once we've got our hands on the right data, it's time to choose our artistic medium... uh, I mean, visualization technique. Think of it like selecting the right brushstroke for a painting. We've got options galore: bar charts, line graphs, scatter plots, and heat maps. Each technique has its own superpower, and we need to pick the one that showcases our insights in the most impactful way.

And here comes the design! Don't underestimate the importance of aesthetics in data storytelling. Just like a stunning outfit can turn heads, an eye-catching visual can make your audience stop and take notice. So, think about colors, fonts, and layout - all those elements that make your visuals visually appealing and satisfying to the eye. Remember, we want to strike a balance between looking good and conveying the data effectively.

Now that we've got our SQL-driven visuals all dressed up, it's time to weave them into a narrative. A compelling data story has a clear beginning, middle, and end - just like a rollercoaster ride that takes your audience on an unforgettable journey. You want your visuals to flow seamlessly, guiding your audience through the insights you've derived from the data. It's like telling a gripping tale that keeps them on the edge of their seat.

But wait, there's more! Engaging your audience is crucial. SQL-driven visuals are great, but you also need to cater to your audience's needs and preferences. Tailor the visuals and the narrative to make them relatable and meaningful. Give your audience space to explore and interpret the data themselves, encouraging interaction and feedback. After all, data storytelling is a two-way street.

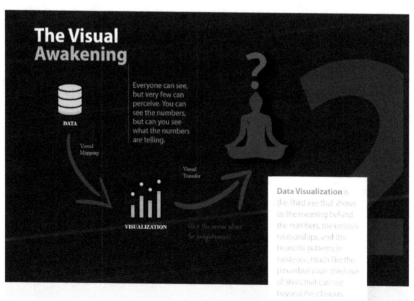

Credit : Ratnesh Pandey

As we venture forth, remember that data storytelling is an ever-evolving skill. Just like a symphony conductor perfects their craft over time, we too can fine-tune our storytelling abilities. Embrace the feedback, iterate, and refine your visuals and narrative. Keep striving for that perfect harmony between data and storytelling.

To wrap it all up, SQL-driven visuals are the ultimate tools to transform raw data into impactful stories. With SQL as our secret weapon, we can unleash the power of data and captivate our audience like never before. So, let's embrace the art of storytelling and watch as our data sings in harmony with the symphony of SQL-driven visuals.

CHAPTER 7

SQL CADENZAS – ADVANCED ANALYTICS

Common Table Expressions (CTEs)

I have been working as a data analyst for quite some time now, and let me tell you, I've always been on the lookout for tools and techniques that can take my data analysis game to the next level. And you know what? One tool that has always caught my attention and proven to be a game-changer for me is the Common Table Expressions (CTEs) in SQL.

Now, CTEs, as the name suggests, are temporary tables that allow us to manipulate data within a single query. They are like these self-contained little powerhouses that bring a whole new level of benefits to the world of data analytics.

One thing that really stands out about CTEs is how they can improve the performance and readability of our queries. You see, by breaking down a complex query into smaller, more manageable sections, CTEs make it much easier to understand and debug. Plus, you can use CTEs multiple times within the same query, so there's no need for redundant subqueries.

Recursive CTE for Hierarchical Data:

But that's not all. CTEs also give us the flexibility to create recursive queries, which are super useful when you're dealing with hierarchical data structures. A recursive CTE is basically a CTE that references itself within its own definition, and it's like the key to unlocking hierarchical information in a concise and efficient manner.

Speaking of hierarchical data, let me tell you, it's everywhere. From organizational hierarchies to file systems to genealogies, you name it. And working with hierarchical data can be a real challenge without the help of recursive queries. Luckily, recursive CTEs provide a simple yet powerful solution.

Let's take a look at an example. Imagine we have a table representing an organizational hierarchy, with each row containing an employee's ID, name, and their manager's ID. With a recursive CTE, we can retrieve a hierarchical representation of the organization, starting from the CEO and going all the way down to the lowest level employees. It's like building a virtual map of the organization in just a few lines of code.

So how does it work? Well, first, we define the anchor member of the CTE, which is like the starting point of our recursion. In this case, it's the CEO(s) - those employees who don't have a manager. We can easily identify them by filtering for rows where the manager ID is null.

Next, we define the recursive member, which is the step that keeps building on the previous iteration. It's like we're joining the CTE with the original table based on the manager ID, so we can keep moving through the hierarchical structure. And we keep doing this until we reach the lowest level employees, where the recursive member returns no more rows.

And voila! We select the required columns from the CTE and do any additional aggregations or transformations we need. And just like that, we have a clear and accurate representation of the organizational hierarchy, ready for further analysis or reporting. It's like we've unlocked a whole new world of insights.

Suppose you have a table representing an organizational hierarchy with columns like EmployeeID, Name, and ManagerID. You can use a CTE to create a hierarchical representation of the organization. Here's an example of how to use a CTE to retrieve the hierarchy, starting from CEOs (employees with no managers):

```
WITH RecursiveCTE AS (
    SELECT EmployeeID, Name, ManagerID
    FROM YourHierarchyTable
    WHERE ManagerID IS NULL -- Anchoring with CEOs
    UNION ALL
    SELECT e.EmployeeID, e.Name, e.ManagerID
    FROM YourHierarchyTable e
    INNER JOIN RecursiveCTE r ON e.ManagerID = r.EmployeeID
)
SELECT * FROM RecursiveCTE;
```

This recursive CTE creates a hierarchical structure, starting from CEOs and expanding to lower-level employees.

But wait, there's more! CTEs have so many practical applications in the world of data analytics. Let me walk you through a few of them.

Periodic Report with CTEs:

First, let's talk about generating periodic reports. Whether it's monthly sales summaries or quarterly performance reviews, CTEs are lifesavers. They allow us to break down the complex logic of the report into smaller, more manageable sections. It's like untangling a messy knot of information and turning it into a neat and organized report.

For example, let's say we want to generate a monthly sales summary, including the total sales for each product category. With CTEs, we can define multiple CTEs that calculate intermediate results like monthly sales by product category, total sales, and average sales. We can then join and aggregate these CTEs to create our final report, which gives us a clear picture of the company's sales performance.

Let's say you want to generate a monthly sales summary report. CTEs can help break down the complex logic into manageable parts. For example, you can use CTEs to calculate monthly sales by product category, total sales, and average sales, and then join them to create the final report:

```
WITH MonthlySales AS (
    SELECT    ProductCategory,    SUM(SalesAmount)    AS
MonthlyTotal
    FROM SalesData
    WHERE Date >= '2023-01-01' AND Date < '2023-02-01'
    GROUP BY ProductCategory
)
SELECT ProductCategory, MonthlyTotal
FROM MonthlySales;
```

In this example, the CTE "MonthlySales" calculates monthly sales by product category.

Clickstream Analysis with Recursive CTE:

Next, let's dive into analyzing clickstream data. Now, clickstream data is like this intricate web of user interactions with a website or application. And navigating through this web requires some serious horsepower. Enter recursive CTEs. They offer us an elegant solution for deriving valuable insights from those hierarchical sequences of events.

So imagine we have a table with clickstream data, including the user ID and the page visited at each timestamp. With a recursive CTE, we can create a hierarchical structure of the user's journey through the website, starting from the landing page and continuing with each subsequent page visit. This hierarchical representation is like a treasure map that helps us identify patterns, conduct funnel analysis, and optimize the user experience.

If you have clickstream data, a recursive CTE can help build a hierarchical structure of user interactions. Consider a table with columns User, Timestamp, and PageVisited:

```
```
WITH RecursiveCTE AS (
    SELECT User, Timestamp, PageVisited, 1 AS Step
    FROM ClickstreamData
    WHERE Step = 1 -- Anchoring at the first page visit
    UNION ALL
    SELECT c.User, c.Timestamp, c.PageVisited, r.Step + 1
    FROM ClickstreamData c
    INNER JOIN RecursiveCTE r ON c.User = r.User AND
c.Timestamp > r.Timestamp
)
SELECT User, PageVisited, MAX(Step) AS MaxSteps
FROM RecursiveCTE
GROUP BY User, PageVisited;
```
```

This recursive CTE creates a hierarchical structure showing user journeys and the number of steps taken.

Data Transformation and Cleansing:

And last but not least, let's talk about data transformation and cleansing. Before we can even think about analyzing data, we often need to clean it up and transform it into a usable format. And let me tell you, CTEs are here to make our lives easier.

Take, for example, a raw dataset containing customer information. It's like a messy jumble of names, addresses, and contact details. But fear not, CTEs can come to the rescue. We can define separate CTEs to handle different aspects of data cleansing, like removing duplicates, standardizing addresses, and validating contact information. Each CTE focuses on one specific task, making our code clear and organized.

CTEs are useful for data transformation. Let's say you have a raw customer dataset that needs cleaning and standardization:

```
WITH CleanedData AS (
    SELECT DISTINCT Name, StandardizeAddress(Address) AS
CleanedAddress
    FROM RawCustomerData
)
SELECT Name, CleanedAddress
FROM CleanedData;
```

In this example, the CTE "CleanedData" removes duplicate records and standardizes addresses.

By harnessing the power of CTEs in this way, we can make our data analysis more efficient and accurate. We can uncover reliable insights that lead to informed decision-making. It's like we're unlocking the true potential of our data.

So there you have it. CTEs are like these unsung heroes of data analytics. They improve query performance, make our code more readable, and give us the power to conquer hierarchical data. Whether it's generating reports, analyzing clickstream data, or transforming and cleansing our data, CTEs are our secret weapon.

Advanced SQL Techniques

Alright, folks, let's dive into the wonderful world of data analysis! One thing that's absolutely crucial in this game is being able to mold your data into a shape that suits your analysis needs. That's where the mighty pivot and unpivot operations in SQL come into play. These bad boys give you the power to reshape your data, leading to deeper insights and smarter decision-making.

Imagine you've got a dataset with columns that represent different categories or dimensions of data. Now, the pivot operation comes in and works its magic. It spins those categories into separate columns, making it a breeze to analyze and compare values across them. On the flip side, the unpivot operation does the exact opposite. It takes those separate columns and stacks them up into one, creating a more compact representation of the data. Talk about transformation!

Pivot Operation

Let me paint you a picture with an example. Picture a dataset that's all about a company's sales across different regions and years. The original structure might include columns for region, year, and sales amount. But, if you want to dig into the sales trends across regions over time, it'd be handy to have separate columns for each region. That's where the pivot operation swoops in like a hero.

With the pivot operation, I can take that original dataset and twist it into a new table with columns for each region. Each column comes with the corresponding sales amounts for each year. And just like that, I can easily compare sales across regions and sniff out any trends or variations. It's like conducting a symphony of insights, harmonizing the data for my analytical pleasure.

Pivoting and unpivoting data is like rearranging musical notes to create different tunes. It's a technique used when your data is not in the right shape for analysis. Pivoting allows you to transform rows into columns, while unpivoting does the opposite.

Hands-On: Pivoting Data
Suppose you have a table of sales data by region, and you want to pivot it to show sales by quarter as columns.
```
```
SELECT Region, [Q1], [Q2], [Q3], [Q4]
FROM (
    SELECT Region, Quarter, Sales
    FROM Sales
) AS Source
PIVOT (
    SUM(Sales)
```
```

```
   FOR Quarter IN ([Q1], [Q2], [Q3], [Q4])
) AS PivotedSales;
```

In this example, we pivot the data to show sales by quarter, making it easier to analyze and visualize.

Hands-On: Unpivoting Data

Conversely, if you have data in a pivoted format and want to return it to its original shape, you can use the UNPIVOT operation.

```
SELECT Region, Quarter, Sales
FROM PivotedSales
UNPIVOT (
   Sales FOR Quarter IN ([Q1], [Q2], [Q3], [Q4])
) AS UnpivotedSales;
```

This technique is like adjusting the notes in a musical composition to create different melodies.

Temporary Tables and Table Variables

Now, let's move on to another neat SQL trick: temporary tables and table variables. These babies can be a lifesaver when you're facing complex queries or calculations that involve multiple steps or intermediate results. They give you the power to store and manipulate data within a session or specific scope, all without creating permanent tables in the database. Talk about convenience!

Temporary tables are just what they sound like—tables that exist temporarily and automatically disappear at the end of a session or transaction. You can create and fill them with data just like regular tables. Plus, they can even have indexes and constraints, which makes retrieving and manipulating data a whole lot more efficient.

Table variables are like temporary tables' close cousins, but they have a few differences. You declare them using the DECLARE statement and typically use them within a single batch or procedure. Table variables can hold data in memory and offer similar capabilities as temporary tables, like column definition and data manipulation. However, they might not be the most efficient option for handling large datasets since they lack support for indexes or constraints.

Both temporary tables and table variables give you the power to break down those complex problems into bite-sized pieces. You can analyze step-by-step and construct queries that build on those intermediate results. These techniques allow you to orchestrate a true symphony of data manipulation and analysis, extracting meaningful insights from the most complicated datasets.

Hands-On: Using Temporary Tables
Imagine you need to perform a complex data transformation involving multiple steps. Temporary tables can help you break the process into smaller, more manageable pieces.
```
-- Create a temporary table
CREATE TABLE #TempData (ID INT, Name VARCHAR(50));

-- Insert data into the temporary table
INSERT INTO #TempData (ID, Name)
SELECT ID, Name FROM OriginalData WHERE Condition = 'X';

-- Perform operations on the temporary table
SELECT * FROM #TempData;

-- Drop the temporary table when you're done
DROP TABLE #TempData;
```

This approach simplifies complex data analysis by allowing you to work on smaller, intermediate datasets.

Time-Series Analysis

But what about time-series analysis? Ah, this is where SQL really starts to sing a sweet melody. Time-series analysis is all about examining data collected over a specific period or at regular intervals. It's incredibly important in fields like finance, economics, and forecasting. Luckily, SQL has a few tricks up its sleeve to make time-series analysis a breeze.

One of the building blocks of time-series analysis is calculating aggregates over time intervals. With SQL's trusty functions like AVG, SUM, and COUNT combined with the GROUP BY clause, you can get aggregate values for specific time periods. Want to know the total sales for each month or the average stock price for each week? No problem, SQL's got your back.

Time-series data is like a rhythmic beat in the music of your analytics. SQL can help you analyze data that changes over time, like stock prices, temperature measurements, or website traffic.

Hands-On: Calculating Moving Averages:
A common time-series analysis is calculating moving averages. Let's say you have stock price data, and you want to smooth out the fluctuations to identify trends.
```
SELECT Date, StockPrice,
    AVG(StockPrice) OVER(ORDER BY Date ROWS BETWEEN 4 PRECEDING AND CURRENT ROW) AS FiveDayMovingAvg
FROM StockData;
```
In this example, we use the `AVG` function as a window function to calculate a five-day moving average of stock prices.

And that's not all! SQL also offers a bunch of date and time manipulation functions that let you extract specific components from timestamps or perform date-based calculations. Want to fish out the year or month from a timestamp? Just use the EXTRACT function. Need to calculate the difference between two dates? The DATEDIFF function's got your back. These functions let you analyze trends, spot patterns, and even make predictions based on historical data. Talk about time travel!

But wait, there's more! SQL's got a bunch of window functions that take time-series analysis to the next level. These bad boys work on a subset of rows within a result set and let you calculate moving averages, cumulative sums, and other aggregations over a specific window or frame of data. They give you the power to pull off complex calculations and derive insights that go way beyond simple aggregate values. It's like watching SQL perform a virtuosic solo!

So, SQL offers a whole arsenal of techniques for advanced data analysis. From pivoting and unpivoting to temporary tables and table variables, and even time-series analysis, it's all about orchestrating a symphony of insights. With these tools in your toolbox, you can bring different pieces of data together and create a true masterpiece in the realm of data analytics. So get out there and start conducting your own data symphony!

Stored Procedures and Functions

Let me tell you a little story about stored procedures and functions in SQL. Back in the 1970s, when SQL was just starting to gain popularity, these babies were born. They were created to make life easier for developers by allowing them to bundle up frequently used SQL statements and execute them all at once. It was like a revolution in the world of data analytics - suddenly, developers could streamline their code and be more efficient.

But these stored procedures and functions didn't stop there - oh no, they evolved and became even more versatile over the years. With the fancy modern database management systems we have now, they've become an integral part of SQL programming, offering all sorts of benefits to developers.

So, what's so great about using stored procedures and functions? Well, let me tell you. First of all, they're the masters of encapsulating complex SQL logic. It's like they bundle up a bunch of SQL statements into a neat little code block and tell them to go do their thing. This means less back-and-forth between your database and your application, which improves performance. It's perfect for those times when you have to run the same set of SQL statements over and over again, like when you're doing data analysis or routine maintenance.

But wait, there's more! Stored procedures and functions also promote code reusability. Imagine being able to avoid copying and pasting your code all over the place. With a well-structured stored procedure or function, you can just call it whenever you need to run a specific set of SQL statements. Not only does this save you time, but it also ensures that you're always consistent in your data analytics process. No more inconsistencies, no more headaches - just smooth sailing.

And let's not forget about security. Stored procedures and functions are like your personal bodyguards for your database. By giving the right permissions to users, you can restrict their access to certain parts of your database while still allowing them to run stored procedures and functions. This means your sensitive data stays safe and sound, and nobody can come in and mess with your database structure. It's like having a fortress protecting your data.

But wait, there's even more! Stored procedures and functions also make your SQL more efficient. By taking advantage of the database engine's optimization capabilities, they can make your queries run faster. Plus, by encapsulating your commonly used SQL statements, you have less code to write, debug, and maintain. It's a win-win situation - more efficiency, less work. Who doesn't love that?

Creating a stored procedure is pretty simple. You just define its name, parameters, and the SQL statements you want it to run. Parameters are like the magic keys that let you pass values to your stored procedure and make it do different things depending on what you need. And functions, well, they're a little different.

They're all about returning specific values or even tables. You can use them in select statements to retrieve and process your data. It's like they become a part of your data retrieval team.

Stored procedures are like scripts that you can store in the database. They consist of SQL statements and can have parameters, making them dynamic. You can execute a stored procedure by calling its name, passing parameters, and it will perform the defined actions.

Functions, on the other hand, are designed to return a single value or a table result. They are used within SQL statements to perform calculations or transformations. Functions can be especially handy in `SELECT` statements to retrieve specific values or perform operations.

Stored Procedure:

Here's a simple example of creating a stored procedure that retrieves employee information based on an employee ID parameter:

```
CREATE PROCEDURE GetEmployeeInfo (@EmployeeID INT)
AS
BEGIN
    SELECT FirstName, LastName, JobTitle
    FROM Employees
    WHERE EmployeeID = @EmployeeID;
END
```

You can call this procedure with an `@EmployeeID` value, and it will return the corresponding employee's information.

Functions:

Here's an example of a simple function that calculates the age of a person based on their birthdate:

```
```
CREATE FUNCTION CalculateAge (@Birthdate DATE)
RETURNS INT
AS
BEGIN
    DECLARE @Age INT;
    SET @Age = DATEDIFF(YEAR, @Birthdate, GETDATE());
    RETURN @Age;
END
```
```

You can use this function in a `SELECT` statement to retrieve ages of people from a table:

```
```
SELECT Name, CalculateAge(Birthdate) AS Age
FROM Persons;
```
```

In this case, the `CalculateAge` function is part of the data retrieval process, providing you with the age for each person.

So, in summary, stored procedures are like customizable SQL scripts with parameters for various tasks, while functions return specific values or tables, often integrated into `SELECT` statements to enhance data retrieval and processing. Both are valuable tools in SQL for different purposes.

So there you have it - the thrilling tale of stored procedures and functions in SQL. They're like the knights in shining armor for developers, helping them build efficient and maintainable code. They improve performance, promote code reusability, and enhance security. And let's not forget about the optimization and faster data retrieval they bring to the table. If you're a data analyst or a developer looking to make magic happen in the SQL Symphony, you better get to know these stored procedures and functions. Trust me, they're the heroes you've been waiting for.

Triggers for Real-time Actions

We're about to embark on an exciting journey into the realm of triggers. We'll explore their inner workings, potential applications, and how they can completely revolutionize the way we analyze and manipulate data. But before we dive into the nitty-gritty details of triggers, let's lay down a solid foundation by understanding their historical progression.

So, triggers in SQL have come a long way since they were first introduced. We're talking late 1970s here when Dr. Michael Stonebraker, the big shot computer scientist, brought this concept to life. Back then, triggers were all about automating tasks in database management systems. Their primary purpose was to tackle data integrity and consistency issues by making sure that any changes made to a database followed the rules and constraints.

Now, these initial triggers were pretty basic. They could only be triggered by specific events like inserting, deleting, or modifying data. Think of them as gatekeepers that would intercept these events and set off the corresponding actions. However, as time passed and the demand for dynamic and responsive applications grew, triggers needed to step up their game.

That's where the 1990s took the spotlight. With the rise of advanced database management systems, triggers transformed big time. They became more powerful, allowing for complex SQL statements, external scripts, and even triggering other triggers. This expansion of functionality opened the doors to real-time analytics and automation, enabling applications to react instantly to changes in the underlying data.

Fast forward to today, and we can see just how essential triggers have become in modern data analytics systems. Their unmatched ability to detect, respond, and automate actions based on data changes makes them indispensable tools for organizations aiming to gain a competitive edge in this data-driven world of ours.

So, let's dig deeper and explore triggers in SQL. These babies are constructs that respond to specific events happening within a database. These events can range from simple data manipulations to more complicated scenarios involving multiple tables or even external events. By using triggers, developers can set rules and define what actions should take place when these events occur.

At a high level, triggers consist of three main components: the triggering event, the conditions, and the actions. The triggering event determines when the trigger fires and can be linked to specific tables or schemas. Conditions establish the criteria that need to be met for the trigger to activate. Finally, the actions define what operations should be performed when the trigger kicks into action.

Now, let me tell you one of the coolest things about triggers - they enable real-time actions. In the old days, data processing and analysis happened in batches, with fixed intervals between events and subsequent actions. But with triggers, that time delay can be minimized or even completely eliminated. Organizations now have the power to develop systems that respond instantly to data changes, providing a truly real-time analytics experience. This opens up a whole new world of possibilities, like fraud detection that requires timely action or automated recommendation engines that adapt on the fly to user behavior.

Triggers can enable real-time actions based on data changes and events in numerous ways. One popular application is data validation and integrity. Triggers act as guardians, ensuring the accuracy and consistency of data by enforcing business rules and constraints. Imagine having a trigger that prevents invalid or duplicate data from sneaking into a particular table - that's data integrity at its finest.

But wait, there's more! Triggers can also automate complex processes involving multiple tables or databases. With the right trigger activation, like an update or deletion, developers can set off a chain reaction of actions that ripple through the system. This not only saves time and effort but also streamlines business processes and boosts overall efficiency.

And guess what? Triggers can go even further by triggering external actions or notifications based on specific data changes or events. Picture this: a trigger sends an email notification whenever a high-value order is placed in an e-commerce system. Or triggers can interact with other systems or produce real-time alerts in response to anomalies or critical events.

You see, triggers offer a kind of flexibility and power that's hard to beat when it comes to enabling real-time actions based on data changes and events. They arm organizations with the ultimate tool to automate processes, ensure data integrity, and create super responsive systems that adapt to changing circumstances on the spot.

But that's not all! Triggers have an even more impressive role: enhancing automation and responsiveness. They take automation to the next level by automatically initiating actions based on predefined rules. Let's say you have a trigger that updates a summary table every time a new row is inserted into a related transactional table - no need for manual intervention, and your summary table is always up-to-date, reflecting the latest data changes.

And what about responsiveness? Triggers come to the rescue by detecting and responding to critical events in real-time. You can design triggers to monitor data changes or patterns and trigger immediate actions or notifications. Imagine having a trigger that analyzes user behavior on an e-commerce platform and generates personalized product recommendations in real-time - talk about impressing your customers!

Bringing it all together, triggers are a crucial part of SQL that enables real-time actions based on data changes and events. From their humble beginnings as simple event-driven mechanisms, triggers have evolved into powerful tools that take automation and responsiveness in data analytics applications to the next level. By using triggers effectively, organizations can create systems that react instantly to changes in the underlying data, allowing for real-time analytics and automation. With their remarkable ability to detect, respond, and automate actions based on data changes, triggers represent a significant leap forward in the field of data analytics, empowering organizations to gain a competitive edge in this ever-evolving world of data-driven decision making.

Let me provide some illustrative examples to showcase their capabilities:

Data Validation and Integrity:

Imagine you're managing a database for an online store. You want to ensure that no invalid or duplicate data is added to the product catalog. You can create a trigger that activates before an `INSERT` statement, checking for data integrity. If the data doesn't meet the predefined rules, the trigger prevents the insertion, ensuring the catalog remains accurate and consistent.

```
```
-- Trigger to ensure data integrity in the product catalog
CREATE TRIGGER PreventInvalidData
BEFORE INSERT ON ProductCatalog
FOR EACH ROW
BEGIN
    IF NEW.price < 0 OR NEW.quantity < 0 THEN
        SIGNAL SQLSTATE '45000'
        SET MESSAGE_TEXT = 'Invalid data. Price and quantity
must be non-negative.';
    END IF;
END;
```
```

Automation of Complex Processes:

Let's consider a scenario where you have an e-commerce system with multiple databases. When an order is canceled, you need to update the inventory, refund the customer, and log the transaction. Triggers can automate this complex process. When an order cancellation is recorded, a trigger can initiate a series of actions across multiple tables and databases, saving time and ensuring the order processing is efficient.

```
```
-- Trigger to automate order cancellation process
CREATE TRIGGER OrderCancellation
AFTER DELETE ON Orders
FOR EACH ROW
BEGIN
    -- Update inventory
    UPDATE Inventory SET quantity = quantity + OLD.quantity
WHERE product_id = OLD.product_id;
    -- Refund the customer
    INSERT INTO Refunds (order_id, amount) VALUES
(OLD.order_id, OLD.total_amount);
    -- Log the transaction
    INSERT INTO TransactionLogs (action, description) VALUES
('Order Cancellation', CONCAT('Order ', OLD.order_id, ' was
canceled.'));
END;
```
```

Real-Time Alerts and Notifications:

In a financial institution, it's crucial to detect and respond to potentially fraudulent transactions instantly. Triggers can be designed to monitor transaction data. When an unusual or suspicious pattern is detected, a trigger can immediately notify the relevant personnel for further investigation or even block the transaction in real-time.

```
```
-- Trigger to detect potentially fraudulent transactions
CREATE TRIGGER FraudDetection
AFTER INSERT ON Transactions
FOR EACH ROW
BEGIN
    IF NEW.amount > 10000 THEN
        -- Send an alert to the fraud detection team
        INSERT INTO Alerts (transaction_id, description) VALUES
(NEW.transaction_id, 'Potential Fraud Detected');
```
```

```
   END IF;
END;
```

Summary Table Updates:

Suppose you maintain a database that logs user activity on a website. You want to generate summary statistics regularly to analyze user behavior. A trigger can be set up to update summary tables whenever new data is inserted. This way, your summary tables are always up-to-date, and you can perform real-time analytics without manual intervention.

```
-- Trigger to update user activity summary
CREATE TRIGGER UpdateUserActivitySummary
AFTER INSERT ON UserActivity
FOR EACH ROW
BEGIN
    -- Update summary statistics
    UPDATE UserActivitySummary
    SET total_visits = total_visits + 1
    WHERE user_id = NEW.user_id;
END;
```

Personalized Recommendations:

In the context of an online retail platform, triggers can analyze user behavior in real-time. When a user browses products, a trigger can generate personalized recommendations instantly, enhancing the user experience and increasing the chances of a purchase.

```
-- Trigger to generate personalized product recommendations
CREATE TRIGGER GenerateProductRecommendations
AFTER INSERT ON UserProductViews
FOR EACH ROW
```

```
BEGIN
  -- Analyze user behavior and generate recommendations
  INSERT INTO ProductRecommendations (user_id, product_id,
  score)
  SELECT              UPV.user_id,              P.product_id,
  CalculateRecommendationScore(UPV.user_id, P.product_id)
  FROM UserProductViews UPV
  JOIN Products P ON UPV.product_id = P.product_id
  WHERE UPV.user_id = NEW.user_id
  ORDER BY score DESC
  LIMIT 5;
END;
```

These examples illustrate how triggers can enable real-time actions based on data changes and events in various scenarios, from ensuring data integrity to automating complex processes, and from detecting anomalies to enhancing responsiveness. Triggers have become essential tools in modern data analytics, offering a level of automation and responsiveness that is indispensable in a data-driven world.

Optimizing SQL for Big Data

So, let's talk about optimizing SQL queries. I'm telling you, it's like fine-tuning a symphony. Getting it right is crucial for the performance of your database system. Lucky for you, there are some techniques that have really hit the spot when it comes to optimizing those queries.

You ready for some optimization magic? Here we go!

Indexing

First up, we've got indexing. It's like a secret weapon. By creating the right indexes, you can make the database system quickly find data based on specific columns. Boom! That means faster query execution. Just take a deep dive into the most frequently used columns in your queries and figure out which indexes to create. You'll be flying through those queries before you know it.

Query Rewriting

Now, let's talk about query rewriting. Sometimes, queries can get pretty complex, am I right? But fear not! By examining the query execution plan, we can identify those suboptimal joins and unnecessary aggregations. And guess what? We can rewrite the query to make it perform better. We break it down into smaller, more efficient parts and watch the magic happen.

Partitioning

Partitioning is another trick up our sleeves. It's like chopping everything into smaller, more manageable pieces. We divide the data based on certain criteria, like range or list partitioning. This makes the database system work on just a subset of data instead of the whole shebang. Can you imagine the time and effort it saves? It's especially handy when dealing with tables that have a gazillion rows.

Caching

Next, we have caching. And let me tell you, it's like having your favorite snacks ready on a shelf. With caching, we store the results of frequently executed queries in memory. So, when we need the same data again, we just grab it from the cache. It's like a shortcut that takes us straight to the good stuff. Time saved.

Normalization

First on the list is normalization. It's all about organizing your data and keeping things tidy. We want to reduce redundancy and dependency, so we eliminate duplicate data and break down tables into smaller, more manageable forms. This not only improves data integrity but also reduces storage requirements. And let's not forget, it boosts query performance, especially for those tables with a hefty number of rows.

But here's the thing, sometimes normalization can slow us down, especially when we're dealing with massive amounts of data. That's where denormalization comes in. It's like adding a little spice to your dish. We selectively reintroduce redundancy into the database structure to optimize query performance. We duplicate certain data and create pre-joined tables to cut out those complex joins. And just like that, we've got faster query execution!

Views

We've got materialized views. It's like having a crystal ball that shows you the future. We create these precomputed tables that store the results of those expensive queries. And then, instead of executing those time-consuming queries repeatedly, we just pull the data from the materialized views. We can refresh them periodically or in real-time, depending on our needs. It's a game-changer, really.

Scaling

Big data means big challenges. But fear not, because we've got some scaling techniques up our sleeves.

Vertical scaling is like upgrading the muscles of your database server. We beef up the hardware, add more memory, or increase the processing power. It gives us an immediate performance boost, which is great, but it does have its limitations when it comes to scalability.

Now, horizontal scaling is where things get interesting. We distribute the workload across multiple database servers. It's like sharing the load with your buddies. We can implement sharding, where each server handles a specific chunk of data. This allows us to add more servers as the workload grows. But hey, it does require some careful management of data distribution and synchronization among servers.

Database Replication

And let's not forget about database replication. It's like having a plan B, ready to go. We create multiple copies of the database, and any changes made to one copy are immediately propagated to the others. This not only improves performance and availability but also gives us that sweet fault tolerance. If the primary server fails, we've got a backup database ready to step in and save the day.

So there you have it, folks. Optimizing SQL for big data is like conducting a symphony. By using techniques like query optimization, database structure optimization, and scaling, we can create a harmonious experience for ourselves and our users. As someone who's been working with SQL and data analysis for a while now, I got to say, these techniques have been a true game-changer for me. And now, I hope they empower you to tackle those big data challenges and unleash the full potential of your SQL-powered systems.

CHAPTER 8

SQL ENCORE – HANDS-ON PROJECTS

Project: Analyzing Sales Data

Alright, folks, buckle up because I'm about to take you on a wild ride through the world of sales data analysis using SQL. Now, I know what you're thinking, "How can analyzing sales data be so crucial?" Well, let me tell you, it's like peeking into the secret lives of your customers, your products, and your overall sales trends. And with SQL by your side, you can transform that raw sales data into some seriously meaningful information that will guide your strategic decision-making like a boss.

First things first, we got to clean up that data. I mean, who wants to analyze a mess? So, we dive into something called data cleansing. Picture this, you've got inconsistencies, errors, and missing values lurking in your dataset, and you're on a mission to hunt them down and fix them. Trust me, as a seasoned data analyst, I've seen it all - duplicate entries, missing values, even inconsistent formatting. But fear not, for SQL queries are here to save the day. These queries help me sniff out those duplicates, using magic like the SELECT statement with COUNT and GROUP BY clauses to group records by unique identifiers like customer name or sales order number. With just a few clicks, I can catch those sneaky repetitions and erase them from existence.

```
```
-- Removing Duplicate Entries based on Customer Name
DELETE FROM your_table
WHERE (customer_name, other_columns) IN (
  SELECT customer_name, other_columns
  FROM your_table
  GROUP BY customer_name, other_columns
  HAVING COUNT(*) > 1
);

-- Handling Missing Values (Assuming NULL values)
UPDATE your_table
SET column_name = default_value
WHERE column_name IS NULL;

-- Correcting Inconsistent Formatting (Example: Making all names
uppercase)
UPDATE your_table
SET customer_name = UPPER(customer_name);

-- Handling Inconsistent Formatting with CASE
UPDATE your_table
SET column_name =
  CASE
    WHEN condition_1 THEN corrected_value_1
    WHEN condition_2 THEN corrected_value_2
    -- Add more conditions as needed
    ELSE column_name
  END;
```
```

The provided SQL samples cover common data cleaning tasks such as removing duplicate entries, handling missing values, and correcting inconsistent formatting. These queries are adaptable to your specific dataset and requirements.

Now that our data is squeaky clean, it's time to mix things up a bit with some data aggregation. We take that beautifully cleansed data and start summarizing and grouping it, so that we can see some real juicy insights at various levels of detail. Imagine analyzing sales trends across different dimensions like time, region, and product category, giving you the power to really dig deep into what's cooking in your business. SQL's got your back with aggregate functions like SUM, COUNT, and AVG, helping you calculate metrics like total sales revenue, average sales quantity, and the number of transactions. And with the GROUP BY clause, you can slice and dice that sales data by a specific dimension, like product category, opening up a world of knowledge about what products are rocking the sales charts. That kind of analysis, can make a real difference in targeting the right customers and managing your inventory like a champ.

```
```
-- Calculate total sales revenue by product category
SELECT   product_category,   SUM(sales_amount)   AS
total_sales_revenue
FROM sales_data
GROUP BY product_category;

-- Calculate average sales quantity by region
SELECT region, AVG(sales_quantity) AS average_sales_quantity
FROM sales_data
GROUP BY region;

-- Count the number of transactions by month
SELECT   EXTRACT(MONTH   FROM   transaction_date)   AS
month, COUNT(*) AS transaction_count
FROM sales_data
GROUP BY EXTRACT(MONTH FROM transaction_date);
```
```

These SQL samples demonstrate how to use aggregate functions like SUM, COUNT, and AVG along with the GROUP BY clause to summarize and group your data by various dimensions such as product category, region, and time. This allows you to extract valuable insights from your data and make informed business decisions.

Alright, we've got some serious insights under our belt, but now we need to show off our hard work. It's time to bring those numbers to life with some data visualization. Because let's be real, complex information can be a real snooze-fest if it's not presented right.

SQL-based visualization tools will make your sales data pop like confetti at a party. Yeah, I know, sounds fun, right? Tools like Tableau and Power BI let you whip up interactive dashboards and reports, all powered by your trusty SQL queries. Think visually appealing charts, graphs, and maps that bring your sales data to life. Want to explore further? No problem. These tools have nifty features like filtering, sorting, and drill-down, so you can dig deep into your data and uncover insights that will blow your mind.

The choice of charts for your data visualization will depend on the specific insights you want to convey. In the context of analyzing sales data and business performance, here are some types of charts that could be highly relevant:

1. ***Line Charts:***
    - Use line charts to show trends over time, such as sales trends by month or year.
    - Visualize changes in key performance metrics, like sales revenue or profit, over a period.
2. ***Bar Charts:***
    - Bar charts are effective for comparing different categories or groups, such as sales by product category or region.
    - Use grouped or stacked bar charts to show the composition of a category, like product sales by region.
3. ***Pie Charts:***
    - Pie charts are suitable for showing the proportion of each category within a whole, like the percentage of sales contributed by each product category.
4. ***Scatter Plots:***
    - Use scatter plots to explore relationships between two variables, such as sales revenue and marketing expenditure.

- This can help identify correlations or outliers in your data.

5. *Heatmaps:*
   - Heatmaps are great for visualizing large datasets. They can show patterns or anomalies, like sales performance across different products and regions.
   - Color coding can help quickly identify high and low values.

6. *Gantt Charts:*
   - Gantt charts are useful for project management and tracking, showing tasks over time, including their start and end dates.

7. *Treemaps:*
   - Treemaps can display hierarchical data, making them suitable for visualizing sales hierarchies like product categories and subcategories.

8. *Area Charts:*
   - Area charts are similar to line charts but can be used to show the cumulative total of a measure over time, such as cumulative sales over months.

The choice of charts should align with the specific insights you want to communicate and the questions you're looking to answer. You can also combine different chart types within a dashboard to provide a comprehensive view of your data. Additionally, interactive features like filters, slicers, and drill-down functionality can enhance the user's ability to explore and understand the data further.

Oh, and did I mention that SQL has its own little secret? Yup, it can do its very own visualizations too. I kid you not. SQL's got charting functions like Bar Charts, Pie Charts, and Line Charts that you can whip up right in your query. So, no need to rely on those external tools if you're in a hurry. SQL's got your back, always.

So, there you have it. Analyzing sales data using SQL is like conducting a symphony of insights. With your solid SQL skills and a deep understanding of data analysis principles, you're unstoppable. Cleanse that data, aggregate it like a boss, and visualize that beauty. With the power of SQL and your analytical mind, your business is bound to reach new heights.

Project: Customer Segmentation

As I reflect on my journey as a software and application developer, I can't help but think about the pivotal role that data analysis played in shaping my understanding of business success. Each project I tackled, I grew more fascinated by the incredible power of data and the valuable insights it held. But what really captured my attention was the world of customer segmentation, a game-changer in the realm of marketing strategies.

Customer segmentation is like peeling an onion – it's about dividing a company's customer base into distinct groups based on certain criteria. By doing so, businesses gain a deeper understanding of their customers and can tailor their marketing strategies to create truly personalized experiences. And let me tell you, the benefits of customer segmentation are mind-blowing. It allows companies to use their resources more efficiently, precisely target specific segments, and ultimately drive revenue growth.

As I dived headfirst into the world of data analysis, I soon realized that SQL, a language I was very familiar with, could be the golden ticket for customer segmentation. SQL, or Structured Query Language for those not in the know, is a programming language designed for managing data stored in relational databases. It's a versatile tool that can handle heaps of data and perform complex queries, making it the perfect companion for my customer segmentation endeavors.

One of the first steps in customer segmentation is defining the criteria for segmentation. It could be based on demographics, purchasing behavior, or psychographics – the key is to find meaningful and actionable criteria to target customers effectively.

Armed with my SQL knowledge, I set out to develop a process that would turn raw data into actionable insights.

The journey started with gathering the necessary data from various sources like transaction logs, CRM systems, and marketing databases. With SQL's superpower of interacting with different databases, I was able to bring these scattered data sources together into one consolidated dataset.

With the data collected, it was time to roll up my sleeves and clean and preprocess the data. This involved getting rid of any inconsistencies, missing values, or duplicates that could throw off the accuracy of the results. Thanks to the robust data manipulation capabilities of SQL, I could efficiently cleanse the data and ensure a strong foundation for the segmentation process.

Once the data was spick and span, it was time to work my magic and transform it into actionable insights using SQL. But first, I had to do some exploratory data analysis to get a complete picture of the customer base. By writing SQL queries to aggregate and summarize the data, I uncovered patterns and trends that would be instrumental in defining segmentation criteria.

For instance, I could use SQL to crunch numbers and calculate customer lifetime value, average order value, and purchase frequency. With this information in hand, I could slice and dice the customer base into different segments based on their purchasing behavior. SQL made it a breeze to group customers into categories like high-value, frequent purchasers, or even those who had fallen off the buying wagon. Understanding these segments allowed businesses to tailor their marketing strategies to meet the unique needs and preferences of each segment.

But here's where SQL truly blew my mind – its ability to integrate external data sources. By merging customer data with demographics or social media data, businesses gain a complete understanding of their customers. This integrated approach opens doors for more accurate and precise segmentation, enabling marketing strategies that truly resonate with customers on a personal level.

As I witnessed the transformative impact of SQL on businesses' marketing strategies, a spark was ignited within me. With data-driven insights, targeted marketing campaigns took off, resulting in higher engagement, conversion rates, and ultimately, customer satisfaction. SQL broke the chains of a one-size-fits-all approach, paving the way for a more personalized, customer-centric strategy.

And here's the cherry on top – SQL's ability to track and analyze customer behavior over time. By consistently rerunning the segmentation process with updated data, businesses could adapt their marketing strategies as customer preferences changed. This agile approach ensured businesses remained relevant and competitive in a fast-moving market landscape.

In a nutshell, SQL is an absolute game-changer in the world of customer segmentation. Its power to turn raw data into actionable insights is a game-changer, enabling businesses to target specific customer segments with laser precision and create unforgettable experiences. SQL unlocks the potential of data and orchestrates a symphony of success and growth. So, if you're ready to dive into customer segmentation, grab SQL and get ready to compose a harmonious melody of customer satisfaction and business triumph.

Project: Real-Time Data Alerts

So, picture this: we live in a crazy fast-paced world where businesses need to stay on their toes and respond to changes in the blink of an eye. I mean, relying on old data just doesn't cut it anymore. We need to have the most up-to-date info at our fingertips and be alerted as soon as something important happens. It could be stocks, website traffic, social media...you name it. And that's where a real-time data alert system comes into play.

Let me take you on a journey of building this bad boy using good ol' SQL. Now, first things first, we had to figure out which data sources we needed. This could be any database or data warehouse where all the juicy info was stored. Once we had that, we had to get down and dirty with the data schema and create tables to hold all that real-time data. It was like building a web of connections, mapping out the relationships between different entities. It was like creating our own data universe!

But wait, there's more! We had to set up the means to capture and process that real-time data. We needed to get those connections in place and implement some fancy ETL processes to extract, transform, and load the data into our shiny new tables. And let me tell you, this step required SQL skills that could handle the massive amount of data coming our way. It was like riding a bull in a rodeo - you had to be quick and precise.

Once we had the data flowing, we needed to define the who, what, when, where, and why of our alerts. We had to dig deep into the data and figure out what triggered us. For instance, if we were into stocks, we needed to know when a certain threshold was crossed or when trading volume hit the roof. It was like playing detective, watching for clues and setting up the perfect trap for those critical moments.

Enter SQL hero mode. We used all the cool functions and operators at our disposal to do some serious calculations and comparisons on the data. And with the magic of SQL queries, we could evaluate the data in real-time and BOOM - trigger those alerts like a boss. We even scheduled the queries to run automatically, keeping our eyes peeled for any anomalies popping up. It was like having a personal assistant constantly scanning the data and giving us a heads-up when things got interesting.

But of course, what good is an alert if you don't get the message in time, right? So, we had to integrate our SQL system with a notification service. There were plenty of options - email, SMS, real-time messaging platforms. We just had to pick the one that suited our project and the user's preferences. It was like finding the perfect delivery service to bring us the juiciest news.

All in all, building this real-time data alert system was one hell of a ride. We had to dive deep into the world of SQL and understand how it all ticked. From designing the data schema, capturing and processing the real-time data, to defining those game-changing alerts and making sure they got to us without delay. At the end of the day, it was all worth it. We created a powerful system that gave us the upper hand, armed with real-time insights and the ability to make informed decisions. SQL, you never cease to amaze me in the world of data analytics.

CHAPTER 9

SQL IN THE REAL WORLD

SQL Best Practices

O kay, so let me tell you about this game-changing approach to writing SQL code. I'm talking about making it efficient and maintainable, so you never have to struggle again. It's all about following these golden guidelines, .

First things first, we need to give our tables, columns, and other database objects some love and attention. Give them names that actually mean something, names that tell a story. By doing this, we're bringing clarity and readability to our code, which is super important when you're working with a team or revisiting your own code after a while.

Now, indexing is where the real magic happens. It's like giving your database tables some turbocharged engines. You see, indexing helps the database find and fetch data faster, making our queries perform like Olympic sprinters. When choosing what columns to index, think about the queries you use the most and the type of data you're dealing with. Smart indexing can unleash the true power of your SQL code.

But wait a minute, hold the phone! We need to chat about wildcard characters. You know those little rascals that like to wreak havoc? Be careful where you put them in your queries. Putting wildcards at the beginning can ruin the party. They stop the database from using any existing indexes, sluggish performance guaranteed. Stick them at the end instead, so the database can work its magic efficiently.

Let's take a step further and break down those complex queries. I'm talking about slicing and dicing them into smaller, more manageable pieces. This not only makes our code easier to read but also reduces the risk of errors and messy inconsistencies. Plus, modular code is a piece of cake to maintain and update, saving us precious time and effort in the long run.

Let's talk about SELECT * statements, . I know, it's tempting to grab all the columns from a table, but trust me, resist the temptation. This approach can be a performance nightmare, especially when dealing with massive amounts of data. Instead, play it smart and explicitly specify the columns you need in the SELECT statement. Let's keep things lean and mean!

Data integrity is a big deal, and we need to treat it like royalty. Constraints are our knights in shining armor. Primary keys, foreign keys, check constraints – they're all here to ensure our data stays consistent and reliable. By making use of these constraints, we can stop invalid data from barging in and maintain the accuracy and integrity of our precious data.

Errors and exceptions, they're like those unexpected guests that show up uninvited. But don't worry, we can handle them like a pro. Implement proper error handling mechanisms, like those TRY-CATCH blocks, to gracefully deal with those surprises. This not only makes the user experience better but also helps us troubleshoot and debug like a boss.

Keep your code at its peak performance by optimizing it regularly. It's like taking your car for a service; we want it running smoothly. Analyze query execution plans, pinpoint the bottlenecks, and make those necessary adjustments. And while you're at it, declutter and refactor your code. Get rid of any unnecessary or redundant operations, and watch the performance soar.

So there you have it, . Following these guidelines and recommendations will make your SQL code shine brighter than the sun. It's like conducting a symphony of data analytics, each piece coming together harmoniously. Embrace the beauty of efficient and maintainable code, and your data will sing with accuracy and performance. Get ready to unlock the true potential of SQL, . It's time to let your code and data dazzle.

SQL in Different Industries

Let me tell you about SQL. Now, I know finance may not be the most captivating topic out there, but trust me, it's got its own kind of excitement. See, in the world of finance, everything revolves around data. And that's where SQL comes in. It's like the backbone of the financial industry, helping professionals like me manage and analyze mountains of complex data. We use it to handle customer transactions, calculate financial ratios, and make smart investment decisions. SQL is like our secret weapon, letting us navigate through the ever-changing landscape of finance.

But it's not just finance that benefits from SQL. Take healthcare, for example. They deal with massive amounts of data too, especially with all those electronic health records. With SQL, healthcare providers can easily retrieve and update medical records, improving patient care and streamlining operations. They can analyze patient demographics, diagnose diseases, and even monitor treatment outcomes. It's helping them make breakthroughs in critical research and keeping us all healthier.

Now, let's talk about e-commerce. You know those online retailers that seem to know exactly what you want? Well, they're using SQL to do it. They manage their inventories, track sales, and analyze customer behavior all with the help of SQL. It's like a superpower for businesses, letting them identify trends, understand preferences, and optimize pricing. Thanks to SQL, they can create personalized marketing campaigns that make you feel like they've read your mind.

And don't even get me started on the travel and hospitality industry. They've got reservations, bookings, and customer interactions to juggle. But with SQL, they can seamlessly integrate all that data and make the whole process smooth as silk. They're able to customize offers based on customer preferences, track satisfaction ratings, and make your travel experiences unforgettable. It's like the magic behind the scenes that makes your dream vacation a reality.

But it doesn't stop there. SQL is a true chameleon, fitting into all kinds of industries. Take manufacturing, for example. They use SQL to manage production processes, track inventory, and keep supply chains in check. Telecommunications companies rely on it to analyze customer usage patterns and optimize network performance. And even in education, SQL supports systems like student information and course management. It's streamlining administration and helping researchers make breakthroughs.

In the end, SQL is like the glue that holds the data analytics world together. It's flexible, powerful, and efficient, making it an indispensable tool for managing massive amounts of data. And as technology keeps evolving, you can bet that SQL will stay at the forefront, shaping the future of information management and decision-making across industries. So, whether you're crunching numbers in finance or exploring new frontiers in healthcare, SQL is your go-to companion. Trust me, it's a game-changer.

Career Paths in SQL and Data Analytics

Alright, let's get real and talk about SQL and data analytics. If you're scratching your head wondering what these terms even mean, don't worry, I got you covered. So, SQL stands for Structured Query Language, which basically means it's a programming language used to handle and pull information from relational databases. It's like the secret code that helps us manage all that juicy data. On the other hand, data analytics is all about digging deep into those massive volumes of data to uncover hidden gems of information and make smart decisions based on that.

Now, picture this: we're living in a world that thrives on data-driven insights. Every industry out there is jumping on the SQL and data analytics bandwagon to gain a competitive edge. And you know what that means? It means the demand for professionals who can rock these tools and crunch numbers like nobody's business is skyrocketing. That's why we're here to explore the cool career opportunities waiting for you in the SQL and data analytics realm.

First up, we have the data analyst. This is one hot role, . As a data analyst, you get to be the hero who collects, analyzes, and interprets data to help organizations make those oh-so-important decisions. You got to have ninja-level skills in SQL, and you better be fluent in data analysis techniques and tools. Plus, being a smooth talker who can translate all the number mumbo jumbo into plain English for the big shots is a must.

Next on the list is the business intelligence analyst. Think of this role as a super-sleuth who investigates data to find golden nuggets of wisdom. You work closely with different folks to figure out what metrics matter, create fancy visualizations, and whip up reports that'll knock their socks off. It's like being a detective, but instead of solving crimes, you're solving business puzzles. And yeah, you got to be a total SQL pro and have a good grasp on data modeling and business intelligence tools.

Now, if you're a tech nerd who loves to dive deep into complex data sets, being a data scientist is your calling. These folks are the Sherlock Holmes of the data world. They use advanced statistical techniques, machine learning algorithms, and fancy programming languages like Python or R to extract the juiciest insights from those big, bad, complex data monsters. A solid foundation in SQL is crucial here, 'cause you need to retrieve and prep the data like a boss.

Let's not forget the mighty database administrators. These guys are the gatekeepers of data integrity, security superstars, and the masters of performance optimization. They ensure those databases are running like a well-oiled machine, and they know SQL like the back of their hand. You'll need to be best buds with things like database management systems and data modeling too.

Last but not least, we have the data engineers. These cool cats are all about designing, developing, and maintaining the infrastructure needed to store and process data. They work closely with data scientists and analysts to build efficient data pipelines, extract data from different sources, and transform it into a format that's ready to be analyzed. And of course, SQL skills are off the charts for these folks, but knowing programming languages like Python or Java is also a HUGE plus.

Alright, those are just a few examples of the amazing career paths you can rock in the SQL and data analytics universe. But here's the deal, : whether you're an analyst, a scientist, an engineer, or a database wizard, there are some core skills you need to ace.

First and foremost, you got to have a strong command of SQL. It's like the foundation of your work. You need to know how to query that data, play with it, and design databases like nobody's business. It's your secret weapon.

Oh, and programming languages? Yeah, those are game-changers too. Python and R are like your sidekicks who make life easier by automating tasks and building predictive models. Trust me, these skills will make you the hero of your team.

Now, let's get nerdy and talk stats. Having a solid foundation in statistics and math is like having a superpower. Understanding concepts like probability, hypothesis testing, and regression analysis will make you the master of extracting meaningful insights from those mind-boggling datasets.

And here's a secret sauce ingredient for success in this field: being a rockstar communicator. Yep, you need to be able to explain your findings to people who may have no clue about all this technical stuff. So, learning how to break down complex information into bite-sized, actionable insights is a skill that'll take you places.

Okay, now it's time for a reality check. The SQL and data analytics field is a constantly evolving beast. Technologies and techniques popping up left and right, and you need to stay on top of the game. Get out there, take courses, get certified, and attend conferences. Keep learning and growing, . That's how you stay ahead of the curve and become an invaluable asset in this exciting, ever-changing industry.

Bottom line? The world of SQL and data analytics is huge, diverse, and ready for you to dive in. Whether you're all about those complex datasets or designing killer database systems, there's a role that suits your interests and skills. The world is craving professionals who can extract insights and make data-driven decisions. So, buckle up, master those SQL skills, dive into programming, stats, and communication, and get ready to rock this thrilling, dynamic field. The opportunities are out there waiting for you.

CONCLUSION

When I first set foot on my SQL journey, I had absolutely no clue about the incredible opportunities that lay ahead. Just like any beginner, I started with the basics - you know, creating tables, inserting data, and digging up information with queries. It was like unlocking a secret world of data manipulation, so captivating that I couldn't fathom the endless possibilities that SQL held.

But hold on tight, because as you dive deeper into the world of SQL, you'll stumble upon advanced topics that will push you to the brink and expand your horizons. One of those topics is database normalization. This fancy term is basically a technique used to eliminate duplication and make database design more efficient. It's like breaking down a massive table into smaller, more manageable chunks that are connected like puzzle pieces. Not only does normalization ensure the integrity of the data, but it also acts as a shield against pesky anomalies and inconsistencies. So buckle up, because understanding and implementing this normalization stuff will supercharge your SQL skills and let you create databases that are efficient and scalable.

Now, here's another topic that'll give you some serious thrills - performance optimization. As databases grow bigger and messier, the quest for speedy query execution becomes a top priority. And guess what? SQL offers a whole arsenal of tools and strategies to make queries fly. One of the big guns is indexing. It's like building a supercharged road map to find exactly what you need with lightning speed. By carefully selecting columns and creating indexes, you can reduce query execution time to a mere heartbeat. And that's not all, . Delving into execution plans, query optimization techniques, and database tuning will give you the power to fine-tune your SQL code and squeeze out every drop of performance from your database system.

But hey, it's not all about cramming your brain with knowledge. You got to keep your finger on the pulse of the latest trends and technologies in the world of data analytics. Trust me, this field is like a living, breathing organism that keeps evolving day in, day out. So, if you want to stand tall and kick some career butt, stay up to date. One of the hottest trends right now is NoSQL databases. They're a whole different breed compared to traditional relational databases. NoSQL is all about handling massive amounts of unstructured or semi-structured data like a boss. It's like having a flexible framework that can adapt to your ever-changing needs. SQL is still a rockstar skill to have, but getting cozy with NoSQL databases like MongoDB or Cassandra will take your career prospects to new heights.

And here's a game-changer for you - the integration of SQL with programming languages. Now, hold your horses, because when you combine the power of SQL with languages like Python, R, or Java, you unleash a whole different level of data magic. These programming languages pack a punch with libraries and frameworks for data manipulation, analysis, and visualization. It's like putting on a superhero cape and transforming into a data superhero. With this combo, you can unlock the full potential of your data and extract insights that'll leave others in awe.

But here's the reality check, . As you continue your SQL journey and delve into advanced topics, never ever forget the importance of continuous learning. The field of data analytics never stays the same, so you got to stay on your game. Go to conferences, workshops, and webinars. Devour books and articles. Dive into online communities and forums. Surround yourself with other SQL enthusiasts who share your passion for unraveling data mysteries.

Constantly challenge yourself and push your boundaries. That's the secret sauce to staying ahead of the curve.

To wrap it all up, SQL is like an eternal symphony that harmonizes the world of data analytics. It beckons us to embark on a journey of learning, exploring, and growing. So my dear reader, as you march on in your SQL journey, remember to embrace those advanced topics like database normalization and performance optimization. Keep your ear to the ground for emerging trends and technologies like NoSQL databases and the magic of SQL programming. And above all, never ever cease to learn. SQL has the command to transform your career and empower you to unravel the deepest insights from your data. So onward, with passion and determination. The symphony awaits.

Your Role in the Data Symphony

Alright, let's talk about the vital role we play in the wonderful world of data analytics. As we dig deeper into the realms of SQL and data analysis, it's crucial to understand just how much power we have at our fingertips.

Data, is the lifeblood of organizations, coursing through every inch of our lives. From the moment we groggily reach for our smartphones in the morning to the interactions we have with businesses throughout the day, data is being collected and analyzed to improve our experiences and guide smart decision-making. And guess what? We're the ones who hold the key to this data-driven kingdom.

"But why is our role so important?" I hear you ask. Well, let me paint you a picture. Imagine we're working for a retail company, right? And this company wants to optimize their inventory management system. They've got stores scattered across various regions, each with its own unique demand patterns. Now, this company collects a mountain of data - sales figures, customer behavior, and other juicy tidbits.

As savvy data analysts, we can process and analyze this data using the magic of SQL. We can uncover gems of insights that will completely transform how this company handles their inventory management. And that's where the power of our role shines through - by understanding just how crucial our work is, we can present killer recommendations that are grounded in cold, hard data.

Let's dive into the nitty-gritty, shall we? Here are some key points to highlight the importance of our role:

1. First things first, we need to fully grasp the power of SQL. It's like the language of data analytics, offering us a nifty way to query, manipulate, and slice through data. It's the foundation for any successful data analysis project. And when we truly master SQL, we gain the superpowers to extract meaningful insights from fickle, complex datasets. That means smarter decisions, .

2. In today's cutthroat business world, organizations live and die by data. And by becoming SQL gurus, we become the champions of data-driven decision-making. Gone are the days of relying on gut feelings and guesswork. No, sir. Our role is to bridge that gap between raw data and actionable wisdom. We use hard evidence to guide organizations in making informed, game-changing decisions.

3. Hey, it's not all about crunching numbers. Data analysis is about problem-solving, - tackling real-world challenges head-on. Our job as aspiring data analysts is to pinpoint those pesky business hurdles and find innovative ways to solve them using data. With the power of SQL and data analytics, we can uncover hidden patterns, spot mind-blowing correlations, and ride the waves of trends. Yeah, we're like data detectives, saving the day with our analytical prowess.

4. Now, let's talk about communication. Listen up, folks - data analysis isn't worth squat if we can't effectively communicate those mind-blowing insights to the right people. Our role is to weave together the complex tapestry of data into compelling stories, painting vivid pictures with numbers. And guess what? That's where SQL and data analytics come in handy. By mastering these

tools, we gain the ability to present our insights in a clear, concise, and captivating way. We give decision-makers the tools they need to take action based on our analysis.

5. Finally, let's learn to embrace change. The world of data analytics moves at a lightning pace. There are always new technologies, tools, and techniques popping up, demanding that we keep our skills razor-sharp. Our role is to be adaptable, always ready to learn and grow. In this data-driven world, those who can ride the waves of change will be the ones who thrive.

So, my fellow data crunchers, let's raise our glasses to the importance of our role in this data-driven universe. We have the power to unlock the hidden magic within data, revealing insights that drive innovation, boost productivity, and leave our competitors in the dust.

Embrace your identity as a data analyst, and take pride in the fact that you can transform data into a masterpiece of insights and opportunities. With SQL and data analytics as our trusty partners, we have the potential to make a lasting impact and shape the future of organizations and industries.

APPENDIX: SQL REFERENCE GUIDE

SQL Syntax Quick Reference

So, you want to dive into the world of SQL, huh? Well, get ready to meet some important characters called keywords. These bad boys have a fancy meaning in the SQL world and you got to respect that. No trying to use them as identifiers, like table or column names, okay? We got SELECT, FROM, WHERE, INSERT, UPDATE, and DELETE, just to name a few. Trust me, knowing these keywords like the back of your hand is going to save you from some serious data headaches.

Let's start with SELECT. This guy is all about retrieving data from a table. You tell it which columns you want, or if you're feeling lazy, just throw in an asterisk and grab them all. For example, if you say "SELECT column1, column2 FROM table_name," it'll fetch those specific columns for you.

Now, meet FROM. It's all about specifying which table you want to get your hands on. Just slide in the table name after FROM and you're good to go. So, with "SELECT column1, column2 FROM table_name," you're retrieving data from the table you specified.

Next up, WHERE. Brace yourself, because this keyword is all about filtering. You want to narrow down your data based on some specific conditions? WHERE's got your back. Just give it a condition that's either true or false, and it'll fetch data that satisfies that condition. So, "SELECT column1, column2 FROM table_name WHERE condition" is going to give you data that matches that sweet, sweet condition you set.

Moving on, we got INSERT. Picture this: you've got an empty table, and you want to add some new rows. INSERT is your go-to keyword for that. Just tell it the table name and the values you want to insert, and bam, it's like magic. For example, "INSERT INTO table_name (column1, column2) VALUES (value1, value2)" will add a shiny new row with those specific values.

Now, let's meet UPDATE. This keyword is all about modifying existing data in a table. Say you want to change something in a specific column? UPDATE's got your back. Just tell it the table name, the column you want to update, and the new value. Easy peasy, right? So, with "UPDATE table_name SET column1 = value1 WHERE condition," you're updating the specified column with the new value for rows that satisfy that condition.

Lastly, we got DELETE. You want to make some room in your table by clearing out some rows? Well, DELETE is your best friend for that. Give it the table name and a condition to determine which rows to delete, and it'll say "adios" to them. So, "DELETE FROM table_name WHERE condition" will erase rows that match your condition.

Now, let's talk about clauses. These bad boys give your SQL statements that extra oomph. They help you limit, sort, group, and join data in all kinds of cool ways. For example, we talked about WHERE earlier. It's all about filtering data based on specific conditions. But we've got more in our clause library.

Meet ORDER BY. This little guy is all about sorting your retrieved data. Want to see it in ascending order? Just throw in ASC. More of a descending kind of person? No problem, just use DESC. Just tell it the column(s) you want to sort by. For example, "SELECT column1, column2 FROM table_name ORDER BY column1 ASC" will give you data sorted in ascending order based on column1.

Then there's GROUP BY. This one's about grouping rows together based on one or more columns. Want to see the distinct values of one column and count the occurrences of another? GROUP BY's got your back. Just tell it the column(s) you want to group, and it'll do the rest. So, "SELECT column1, COUNT(column2) FROM table_name GROUP BY column1" will give you the distinct values of column1 and count how many times column2 shows up for each value.

But wait, we've got HAVING. It's like WHERE, but for groups instead of individual rows. So, you can filter your grouped data based on conditions. Picture this: you want to see the distinct values of column1 and the count of column2 for each value, but only for groups with a count greater than 5? HAVING's got your back. So, "SELECT column1, COUNT(column2) FROM table_name GROUP BY column1 HAVING COUNT(column2) > 5" will give you just that.

Now, let's talk about some common syntax patterns. These patterns are like recipes for SQL statements, allowing you to perform some pretty complex operations on your data.

First up, we got JOIN. It's all about combining rows from multiple tables based on related columns. We've got INNER JOIN, LEFT JOIN, RIGHT JOIN, and more. Just tell JOIN the column that relates your tables, and it'll bring them together. For example, "SELECT column1, column2 FROM table1 INNER JOIN table2 ON table1.column = table2.column" will retrieve data from table1 and table2, based on the matching values in the specified columns.

Next, meet UNION. This pattern is all about combining the results of multiple SELECT statements into one. Just make sure those SELECT statements have the same number of columns and compatible data types, and UNION will do the rest. So, "SELECT column1, column2 FROM table1 UNION SELECT column1, column2 FROM table2" will grab the unique rows from both table1 and table2 and present them to you.

And last, but definitely not least, we have subqueries. These little gems are like queries within queries. You can use them to retrieve data, perform calculations, or filter rows based on values from another table. So, say you want to retrieve data from table1 where column1 matches the result of a subquery on table2? Just tell it "SELECT column1, column2 FROM table1 WHERE column1 IN

(SELECT column FROM table2)," and it's going to give you exactly what you need.

So, SQL is like a symphony where you, the data analyst, are the conductor. By understanding these keywords, clauses, and syntax patterns, you'll be able to create beautiful, efficient SQL statements. And with that, you'll be ready to make some serious data magic happen. So, go forth, my SQL maestro, and embrace the power of SQL Symphony!

Common SQL Functions and Operators

Math Functions:

I want to let you in on a little secret about SQL - it's not just about querying your data. It's about unleashing the full power of math within your queries. I'm talking about math functions. They're like the hidden gems that can perform all sorts of mathematical calculations right in your SQL statements.

Imagine you want to find the average price of a product in a table. Well, you can use the AVG() function to make your life easier. It's like having a math genie at your disposal. Just take a look at this query:

```
SELECT AVG(price) FROM products;
```

See? With just a few lines of code, you can calculate the average price of all your products. It's math magic happening right in front of your eyes.

String Functions:

Now, let's dive into the world of strings. SQL has a whole toolbox of functions that let you manipulate and analyze text strings. It's like having a Swiss Army knife for your data.

One of the most commonly used string functions is CONCAT(). It's like a magician's trick that combines two or more strings into one. Just think about it - you can retrieve the full name of a customer by simply concatenating their first name and last name. It's as easy as pie:

SELECT CONCAT(first_name, ' ', last_name) AS full_name FROM customers;

Boom! You have the full name of your customer right there. It's like putting together pieces of a puzzle to reveal the bigger picture.

Date and Time Functions:

Dates and times are a crucial part of any data analysis. So, it's no surprise that SQL offers a whole range of functions to help you work with them. These functions allow you to extract specific information from date and time values, like pulling rabbits out of a hat.

Let's say you want to know the year when an order was made. Just use the DATEPART() function to extract the year from a given date. It's like using a magnifying glass to zoom in on the details:

SELECT DATEPART(year, order_date) AS order_year FROM orders;

See? By combining SQL and date functions, you can travel back in time and uncover the secrets hidden within your data.

Aggregate Functions:

Now, get ready for a mind-blowing revelation - SQL can not only crunch numbers, but it can also perform calculations on sets of rows and return a single value. It's like a master mathematician solving complex equations in the blink of an eye.

These magic functions are called aggregate functions, and they are super handy. They can count, sum, find the average, maximum, and minimum values in a set of rows. And when paired with the GROUP BY clause, they can create summary reports that reveal insights about your data. It's like zooming out and seeing the big picture.

Let me give you an example. You can use the COUNT() function to count the number of employees in each department. It's like having a human resources department at your fingertips:

SELECT department, COUNT(employee_id) AS employee_count

FROM employees

GROUP BY department;

Now you have the power to understand the dynamics of your workforce. It's like being in control of a well-oiled machine.

Comparison Operators:

We've covered math, strings, and dates. Now it's time for a little bit of logic. In SQL, comparison operators are like the gates that open up the world of possibilities. They allow you to filter and retrieve specific rows from a table based on certain conditions. It's like having a key to unlock hidden treasures.

The most commonly used comparison operators are =, <>, >, <, >=, and <=. They are your companions in the quest for data. Take a look at this query:

SELECT * FROM orders WHERE order_date >= '2021-01-01';

In this magic incantation, the >= operator retrieves all orders from the year 2021 and onwards. It's like having a time machine that takes you straight to the future.

Logical Operators:

Now, let's dive into the realm of complex conditions. SQL gives you logical operators that allow you to combine multiple conditions in WHERE clauses, creating more sophisticated search queries. It's like building a puzzle with interlocking pieces.

AND, OR, and NOT are your trusty companions in this journey. They help you express your desired conditions and retrieve exactly what you're looking for. Let's see an example:

SELECT * FROM products WHERE (price > 100) AND (category = 'Electronics');

In this spellbinding query, the AND operator brings together electronics with a price greater than 100. It's like shining a spotlight on the products you really want.

Null Functions:

Ah, null values - the tricksters of the data world. Dealing with them can be a challenge, but don't worry, SQL has your back. It offers functions like IS NULL and COALESCE() to handle null values effectively. It's like having the tools to tame the wild beasts.

The IS NULL function helps you check whether a specific column contains null values. It's like a detective identifying suspects:

SELECT * FROM customers WHERE phone_number IS NULL;

With this magical query, you can find customers who haven't provided their phone numbers. It's like putting pieces of the puzzle together to uncover hidden truths.

These are just a few examples of the incredible functions and operators that SQL has to offer. They can transform your data analysis process and help you uncover valuable insights. So, don't be afraid to experiment and explore. And in the next chapter, get ready to join us on an adventure through the world of SQL joins. It's a journey full of surprises and revelations.

GLOSSARY

Key SQL Terminology

S QL is like a language of its own, and to understand it, you need to be familiar with its key terms. Let's take a journey through these essential concepts:

1. *Database:* The foundation of SQL, a structured collection of data, neatly organized and stored, serving as the heart and soul of any data-driven application.
2. *Tables:* Think of them as spreadsheets within the database. Rows represent individual records, and columns hold details about each record.
3. *Columns:* Vertical elements in a table, each with a unique name and data type, defining the structure and format of the stored data.
4. *Rows:* Horizontal entries within a table, representing unique instances of data and filling in values for each column.
5. *Primary Keys:* VIP passes for records in a table, ensuring every row can be identified and distinguished, crucial for data integrity and relationships.
6. *Foreign Keys:* Columns connecting to the primary key of another table, bridging data across different sources, enabling data relationships.
7. *Indexes:* Clever data structures that speed up data retrieval by creating ordered lists based on specific column values, crucial for query optimization.

8. **SQL Statements:** Commands in the SQL language that allow you to interact with a database, such as SELECT for data retrieval, INSERT for adding records, UPDATE for modifying data, and DELETE for removing records.

9. **SELECT Statement:** The king of SQL statements, used to retrieve data from one or more tables with various conditions, enabling precise data extraction.

10. **JOIN:** A secret weapon for combining data from multiple tables based on shared columns, creating complex relationships between data sources.

11. **WHERE Clause:** Acts as a superpower, filtering and retrieving records that meet specific conditions, allowing you to focus on relevant data.

12. **GROUP BY Clause:** An amazing tool for grouping rows based on one or more columns, often used with aggregate functions like SUM or COUNT for data analysis.

13. **ORDER BY Clause:** Like a conductor, it sorts the result set in ascending or descending order based on specified columns, ensuring organized data presentation.

14. **DISTINCT Keyword:** A filter for SELECT statements, ensuring only unique values appear in the result set, eliminating duplicate data.

15. **Subqueries:** Queries within queries, performing complex operations like filtering data, retrieving information from multiple tables, or calculating aggregated data.

16. **Views:** Virtual tables that present specific data subsets to users, simplifying complex queries and enhancing data security.

17. **Transactions:** Sequences of SQL statements treated as a single unit, ensuring data integrity, especially in multi-user database environments.

18. **Normalization:** Organizing data to reduce redundancy and dependency, improving data integrity and efficiency by breaking down large tables into smaller, manageable ones.

19. **Denormalization:** Introducing controlled redundancy to boost query performance, particularly useful in data warehousing and reporting systems.

20. **Types of SQL Statements:** DML (Data Manipulation Language) for data manipulation, DDL (Data Definition

Language) for defining and managing database structure, and DCL (Data Control Language) for controlling access and managing privileges.

Mastering these key SQL terms is like holding a secret key to unlock the potential of data analytics and database management. Once you're adept at writing efficient queries, normalizing data, and optimizing performance, you can work wonders in the world of data analytics. So, let's dive in, explore the symphony of SQL, and harmonize the vast realm of data analytics. Get ready to make magic happen!

www.ingramcontent.com/pod-product-compliance
Lightning Source LLC
Chambersburg PA
CBHW071253050326
40690CB00011B/2384